The End of Copycat China

The End of Copycat China

The Rise of Creativity, Innovation, and Individualism in Asia

Shaun Rein

WILEY

Tom Tom,
May life be the best journey ever.
Love, Ba Ba

CONTENTS

PROLOGUE

The stage lights beamed so brightly that I could barely see. I wiped the sweat beading on my brow and squinted to my left, where Dylan Ratigan, the host of his eponymous MSNBC show, sat readying to question me about China's changing economy and the release of my book *The End of Cheap China: Economic and Cultural Trends That Will Disrupt the World.*

On air, Ratigan hulks as a towering presence—physically imposing and unafraid to grill guests. In real life, Ratigan looms even larger, like an NFL linebacker. He rotated his head to gaze at me. The way he looked at me reminded me of a lion stalking prey.

I tried to hide my nerves. I had appeared on television many times before but never from 30 Rockefeller Center in Manhattan, where NBC records shows I had grown up watching, such as *Saturday Night Live.* I could not believe 18 hours earlier I had been home in Shanghai and now sat on the same stage many of the world's famous had sat. I saw Eliot Spitzer, the former New York governor caught frequenting $1,000-an-hour hookers, heading toward a green room to get his microphone. *Was I really in 30 Rock,* I wondered, *or was I dreaming?*

"On air in 3, 2, 1," a stagehand yelled out, and I hurtled back to reality. The show aired a clip of Secretary of State Hillary Clinton musing about China–United States relations. She posed a question: "What happens when an established power and a rising power meet?" Would tensions between the two be inevitable as with Germany and the United Kingdom before World War I, or would the nations create a new paradigm for cooperation among superpowers?

Once I heard Clinton's sound bite, I knew Ratigan would grill me. After all, it was just months before the 2012 presidential elections, and anti-China hysteria was at its zenith. *New York Times* columnist Paul Krugman harped seemingly every day that China was a "bad actor" for manipulating its currency. The only issue Republican and Democratic candidates could agree on was conveniently to blame China for all of America's economic ills.

In the corner of my eye, I saw Ratigan flanked by his three regular guest hosts, former Republican candidate for Congress Krystal Ball, author and cultural critic Touré, and policy wonk Ari Melber, poised to pepper me with tough questions.

Ball did not mince words: "How stable is the government, and how threatened are they by protests?" At the time the 2012 Arab Spring, a wave of uprisings, was in full bloom, and Senator John McCain argued the Spring would come to China sooner or later.

McCain was simply wrong, I answered, pointing out the nonpartisan DC-based Pew Center found most Chinese supported the direction the central government was taking the country. Harvard professor Anthony Saich has also come to similar conclusions in his research. Mounting concerns about local government corruption and pollution needed to be addressed, I told Ball—yet there was no chance of an Arab Spring–style mass movement any time soon.

Melber followed by asking if rising income inequality would cause social instability. Good question—the gap between rich and poor had spread wider, and people who had not yet managed to buy a home were frustrated that property price growth outpaced wage increases.

China's economy had reached a dangerous point, the so-called middle-income trap, I answered. When per capita income hits

$6,000, wage growth tends to stagnate. The rich get richer and the poor get poorer, causing social instability, which is what happened in Thailand and explains why the land of smiles had yet another military coup in 2014. Only a handful of countries, such as Japan, have overcome the trap after World War II. China must spread wealth more or run the risk of failing to develop a stable middle class, the backbone of healthy economies.

To combat stagnation, the Chinese government must enforce labor laws, raise minimum wages, and shift the economy more toward innovation, services, and consumption. More Chinese need access to health care, affordable housing, and a safety net similar to Social Security.

Ratigan pounced, asking whether it was fair to accuse China for "screwing" America with "rigged trade" and intellectual property infringement. At the time China's economy remained robust with 8 percent gross domestic product (GDP) growth, whereas the highest unemployment rates since the Great Depression savaged America.

As I parried Ratigan's and his cohosts' questions, I realized many Americans believe China's 30-year economic growth since its opening up in 1978 was predicated on copying intellectual property, rigging the currency rate, and stealing American jobs.

Few knew about China's moves up the manufacturing value chain, that the currency called the yuan had appreciated more than 25 percent against the U.S. dollar since 2005, or that China was now itself losing light industrial jobs to even cheaper countries, such as Sri Lanka, Indonesia, and Cambodia.

They did not realize Chinese consumers had started shunning Louis Vuitton (LV) knockoffs to become the second-largest global buyers of luxury items and the biggest-spending tourists to America and France per capita. They spent more per capita for the London 2012 Olympics than any other nation. In the meantime, China had become America's second-largest trading partner after Canada and accounted for nearly 30 percent more trade than the European Union.

That day, I pushed back against Ratigan and his cohosts, arguing Chinese consumers had "saved America's agricultural sector by buying corn, nuts, and meat proteins." Without them, America's heartland would be far worse off. By 2013, the U.S. Department of Agriculture announced China was the largest recipient of American agricultural exports, more than $26 billion, up from seventh just a decade before. China's rise also created opportunities for American companies, such as Starbucks and Apple.

After 9 minutes the interview ended. I let out a sigh of relief. Ratigan shook my hand and furnished me a big smile. He has that politician's charisma; he made me feel like I was his best friend. A few months later he walked away from a multimillion-dollar contract and fame at MSNBC to launch hydroponic farming to employ American war veterans. I wouldn't be surprised if he runs for political office in the future.

Fortunately, my book was well received, and organizations from all over the world invited me to discuss its conclusions. The strategic market intelligence firm I started in 2005, the China Market Research Group (CMR), saw business take off as multinationals, private equity firms, hedge funds, and Chinese firms engaged us to understand and develop strategies to deal with the changes occurring.

Over the next two years, I seemed to live in boardrooms, hotels, or airplanes as I keynoted conferences and met with businesspeople in Sydney, Tokyo, San Francisco, Cape Town, Bangkok, Singapore, and New York.

I met dozens of billionaires, hundreds of senior hedge fund investors, and the boards and chief executive officers (CEOs) of the world's largest firms. They all wanted to know the main trends in China and what they meant for business. Few had reliable, current information on what really happened on the ground.

Pundits such as independent economist Andy Xie, former professor at Tsinghua University Patrick Chovanec and former macroeconomist for China for CLSA Andy Rothman had hijacked the media with controversial stands. They manufactured great sound bites but did not offer the nuance needed to make investment decisions. Permabears, analysts who always hold negative opinions toward China's economy and have claimed for years an imminent crash, such as Xie and Chovanec, never seemed to regard positive data whereas Rothman overlooked the very real dangers in the economy emerging.

The truth is the economy is not heading toward disaster—or toward perpetual growth. Reality lies somewhere in the middle, with companies adjusting quickly to changes profiting while lumbering ones go the way of the dodo.

What worked three years ago might not work anymore, and it certainly won't work three years from now. Most executives I met thought the country based growth on heavy investment, exports, and theft of intellectual property—few realized 50 percent of growth in 2013 derived from consumption.

Only a handful were aware that some of the world's most innovative companies—firms such as Alibaba, Tencent, and Lenovo—were Chinese and that many outspent their foreign counterparts on research and development (R&D). In 2013 for instance, telecom maker Huawei invested $5 billion in R&D versus $4.9 billion by Ericson, its major competitor. Many of these had firms had started expanding to Southeast Asia, Eastern Europe, and Africa.

Few executives understood the role of urbanization in kick-starting the economy. Prime Minister Li Keqiang set the goal of reaching a 60 percent urban population in the next five years, up from 30 percent in the 1990s and 52 percent currently. To give context, before it started two decades of stagnation, Japan hit a 90 percent urbanization rate in 1992.

Most urbanization is being pushed into the hundreds of smaller third-, fourth-, and fifth-tier cities few foreigners know, cities such as Shantou, Anshan, and Nanping with populations of more than 1 million, by easing *hukou* (household registration) and home-buying requirements, while limiting population growth in metropolises, such as Shanghai and Beijing.

During meetings, I showed why China's growth model of exporting and building roads to economic success is broken and that innovation, services, and consumption need to account for a larger proportion of growth. The shift is happening but risks abound as local governments have become addicted to growth fueled by cheap credit.

I wrote *The End of Cheap China* to show the country faces an aging population, soaring rents and salaries, and a labor force that wants to realize its white-collar dreams rather than toil away in factories. I argued U.S. companies needed to move up the manufacturing value chain, relocating to other countries or cheaper parts of the nation or potentially reshoring operations to the United States. Reshoring is happening with companies such as the toy manufacturer K'NEX, which is already relocating operations to America. Foxconn, maker of many of Apple's products, has invested billions in Indonesia and Vietnam.

I said it was time to sell into the country. Over the past three years I have been proved right—costs there have continued to rise, squeezing margins, and the China cost advantage no longer really exists in light industry. Thousands of companies have gone bankrupt or lost money, unable to adjust to new realities. Profits for Western firms selling into the country with the right strategies soared, with the nation becoming the largest market globally for companies such as health and beauty multilevel marketer Amway, sports car Porsche, and semiconductor company Qualcomm.

As I traveled I realized the changes and reforms taking place were happening so fast that they were hard for people outside the country to follow. Seemingly every day the government issues new regulations, whether it be liberalizing cash deposits for banks, reducing regulatory oversight for cross-border investments, or even something relatively small, such as extending the inspection validity periods on automobiles from one year to six, but which will change entire industries. Even for people within China, all the changes can be hard to keep up with.

I decided to write this book, *The End of Copycat China,* as a follow-on to show the changes happening in the economy since my last book and to predict the next decade's megatrends to provide a framework for investors and executives.

Slowing growth is the new reality but should not be feared—it shows the government, especially China's new president, Xi Jinping, has finally recognized the need to rein in cheap credit and focus on economic efficiency and is confident enough to do both. Xi has consolidated power, overcome embedded constituencies, and harnessed the bureaucracy to follow his lead to move toward a healthier China. Xi's far-reaching anticorruption campaign to reform the bureaucracy has won support from everyday people, and he has arguably emerged as the most powerful Chinese leader since Mao Zedong.

The changes boil down to two key changes businesspeople and investors must know.

First, Chinese companies no longer just copycat business models from America and Europe. They still grab low-hanging fruit but focus more on innovation. Multinationals must adjust to increased Chinese competition, which no longer competes just with good-enough products at cheap prices but with value and innovation.

Companies such as telecom maker Huawei have taken market share from Ericson and Cisco. Lenovo replaced Hewlett-Packard as the largest maker of personal computers (PCs) in 2013, not just by competing on low price and distribution. Lenovo's chair and CEO, Yang Yuanqing, was the first person from Asia to receive the Edison Achievement Award in 2013, alongside Elon Musk, CEO and product architect of Tesla Motors and CEO and chief technology officer of Space Exploration Technologies (SpaceX).

Other companies acquire technology by scooping up Western firms, as automaker Geely did with Volvo.

Second, Chinese consumers no longer slavishly copy trends from America and western Europe, or even their own peers in China. The movement to define the Chinese dream and renewed pride in Chinese culture has resulted in consumers moving away from images portrayed in Western advertisements. A high price tag and big flashy logos won't work anymore as marketing and sales strategies. Brands need to truly segment target markets and understand hopes, dreams, and aspirations.

Rampant pollution and unaffordable housing prices have made middle-class Chinese reprioritize what is important and how to spend money. They have gravitated toward niche, authentic, understated brands and experiences. Formerly dominant brands, such as sportswear company Adidas and luxury player LV, must adjust strategies or else China could drag on growth. Changes also mean opportunities for brands to carve out profitable niches, including premium sportswear brand Michael Kors or outdoor apparel company North Face.

Brands need look no further than titans, such as food giant Nestlé, to see how failing to adjust quickly to evolving consumer trends devastates bottom lines and careers. Nestlé lost its China head in 2014 under the cloud of poor performance against fiercer competition from formidable domestic players, such as Kunlun Mountain water in its bottled water division or Yili in ice cream, that were nimbler in launching new products.

This book is an effort to show these changes up close and to provide a framework for businesspeople to prepare for these changes. Chinese firms and the Chinese government focus on innovation, the application of improved solutions to meet market demand with better processes, technologies, services, and ideas. Innovation differs from invention, which is the creation of the idea or method in the first place.

Known more for rampant piracy, state domination of the economy, and a heavy regulatory hand that stifles innovation, China might surprise by how much it is starting to evolve. Innovation is becoming part of the discourse, consumers are shunning *shanzai* (knockoffs and imitations), and the government is starting to encourage, rather than stifle, innovation.

China is progressing along an innovation development curve from:

1. Copycat stage, to
2. Innovation for China stage, where it is now mostly, and from here to
3. Global innovation stage, where China begins innovation for the rest of the world, already partially underway in some sectors, such as mobile devices and services.

The impetus for the shift toward stages 2 and 3 is being driven by Chinese consumers who want the best products and services developed for them directly and by ambitious, well-capitalized companies looking to offset a slowing, more competitive economy by becoming global players.

To get that up-close vantage point, I interviewed everyday consumers, business executives, billionaires, and founders of some of China's most innovative and most profitable firms. I even talked to officials—including some heads of state—of countries that have dealt closely with the Chinese government to provide a macro-level view. I also relied on more than 50,000 surveys of consumers my firm, CMR, has conducted.

Case studies of winning and failing companies are included to provide concrete knowledge of what works and what doesn't.

The chapters of this book are grouped into four sections based on the three stages of China's innovation development curve:

1. For most Chinese companies in the past 35 years, little reason existed to try to be innovative or even to build brands. Growth relied on heavy investment and low-hanging fruit dangled enticingly, incentivizing companies to copycat other successes, focus on the short term, and make a quick buck. Facing rapid growth and lack of property rights, Chapters 1 and 2 will show Chinese companies did not look at the long-term picture and viewed investing in innovation as too expensive and risky—and so did private investors.

2. The low-hanging fruit in China's economy is now disappearing as competition and costs rise. Executives are becoming focused on the long term, seeing profits derive from innovation for China specifically, stage 2 on the innovation curve. Much of the innovation currently can be defined as business model rather than technological innovation. Chapters 3 and 4 will examine what sectors see the most innovation and how far along they are toward achieving stage 3, where companies innovate for the rest of the world. This section will also look at what barriers and challenges, such as a weak education system

that focuses too much on rote memory, exist that hamper the pace of innovation.

3. As Chinese redefine the ideal Chinese dream, they are changing what they spend their money on. Chapters 5 through 9 will examine shifting spending patterns and how renewed patriotism is affecting their purchasing habits. I will look at how mobile, e-commerce, food and beverage, tourism, and entertainment and leisure sectors will continue to rise whereas the department store, luxury, apparel, and footwear sectors will face challenges and how companies can overcome the obstacles.

4. In the last part of the book, Chapter 10, I will look at how the changes in China's economy will affect Cambodia, Indonesia, and other nations in Asia, such as how factories relocating to Indonesia will help create its own emerging middle class, yet tension with nations such as Japan, the Philippines, and Vietnam is bound to increase.

China's continued economic success is not guaranteed. Rising nonperforming loans, weakening middle-class consumer confidence, and tension with neighbors could slow or even halt its economic rise.

The only thing guaranteed about China is that it is changing fast and that its shifting economic growth will affect and disrupt the rest of the world—it is no longer a copycat nation. To find out where the nation is going, we have to see where it once was, and that is where I will start the book.

1

THE INNOVATION CURVE STAGE 1

COPYCAT COMPANIES AND LOW-HANGING FRUIT

I t was 2007. I was asked to moderate a one-on-one keynote interview with Jason Jiang, the billionaire founder of NASDAQ-listed darling Focus Media, for *Advertising Age*'s annual conference in Shanghai.

Focus Media was a big deal in advertising; the company's looping series of ads on digital screens had become ubiquitous. When it had gone public two years before in 2005, it became the largest Chinese initial public offering (IPO) ever on the NASDAQ exchange, raising $172 million before its greenshoe option, which is when the underwrite is allowed to sell investors more shares than originally planned, which usually happens when the demand is high. Over the next 24 months the shares kept soaring, making

Jiang a staggering fortune. In 2008 *BusinessWeek* estimated Jiang's wealth at $1.8 billion, more than hotel chain heir John Marriott Jr.

Advertising Age's China head at the time, Normandy Madden, informed me that Jiang liked to control conversations and had an outsized personality. Madden confided she asked me to moderate because I was the only person she knew who could stand up to him. She wanted me to ask tough questions and not let Jiang dominate the discussion. "Don't back down," she said.

I reached out to Focus Media's head of marketing, Celia Tong, to arrange a lunch so that Jiang and I could get to know each other. Tong told me Jiang was confident but down-to-earth and liked to talk. Somewhat quirkily, she said Jiang loved foot massages. She also made a point of saying she had never sold a share of Focus Media stock because she believed in Jiang and his vision.

We met at a Shanghai restaurant that was a converted old villa in the city's French Concession, now wedged between two enormous construction sites. What had once been a quiet, genteel neighborhood for the moneyed elite was now a riot of jackhammer noises and grit and dust swirling in the air.

When I entered the private dining room, the slightly doughy Jiang stood up, shook my hand, and immediately started telling me his plans for Focus Media to dominate the advertising sector.

As the server brought over a mound of honey-glazed spareribs accompanied by a tangy sauce on the side, Jiang laid out his plans with the passion of a Pentecostal preacher.

"I want to be number one," he said bluntly. By the time we met, Focus Media was already the country's second-largest media company in terms of advertising revenue after the state-owned television network, CCTV. But Jiang wanted more, he stressed. His goal: to overcome CCTV to become the largest player. For a man who earned a few hundred dollars a month a couple of years before as an ad executive to become one of the world's richest men, anything seemed possible, even toppling CCTV's dominance.

Jiang grew animated as he revealed his plans to grow through acquisitions—he plotted to scoop up online advertising firms and companies in the mobile space. *Did he have a real growth plan*, I wondered, *or was acquisition the scheme*? I thought of Dennis Kozlowski, the former chief executive officer (CEO) of Tyco International that *BusinessWeek* named as one of the top 25 managers to watch in 2001. Between 1991 and 2001 he purchased more than 1,000 companies. Eventually he was jailed for receiving $81 million in unauthorized bonuses, even expensing half of a $2 million fortieth birthday bash for his wife.

Kozlowski became the poster boy for hiding fraud by acquiring so many companies that investors could not make sense of the records.

I wanted to test Jiang's plans. Would he end up like Kozlowski, acquiring companies for nefarious purposes, or would he use acquisitions, like Mark Zuckerberg at Facebook does, to complement core businesses and increase shareholder value?

As the server brought over a mound of steamed vegetables heaped with garlic, I asked Jiang about the effectiveness of Focus Media's core wall-mounted-screen advertising platform and the high installation hardware costs. He gazed at me, slightly bewildered, and said, "Yes, and I want to buy more companies to get bigger."

I was surprised Jiang did not seem to have a good answer. Was he so addicted to short-term, top-line growth that he did not care about sustainable growth?

As for hardware, he explained the screens and underlying technology were cheap and could last for five years or more. He did not think costs were an issue because everything in China was cheap then.

When changing ads, employees actually went from screen to screen and updated the commercial loops manually, using universal serial bus (USB) sticks—already ancient technology. Labor costs were still low enough that it was cheaper to use workers than develop an automated updating process.

As I left lunch, Jiang shook my hand and said we should grab a foot massage sometime. I left confused. Focus Media had a real business with real paying clients, and Jiang himself was brilliant. However, I was not sure if the business was sustainable. *Does it matter for Jiang or his early financial backers?* I thought. He had already made them all billions using basic technology.

Although not innovative, Jiang got rich by setting up an easy-to-understand business Western investors intuitively got—digital-screen posters in office buildings. Focus Media's model was similar to JCDecaux's billboards and posters that lined highways and airports, except Focus Media's advertising signs were digital.

Focus Media could leverage technology to generate more revenue per footprint by looping a series of TV commercials instead of just a single still image for one brand. More ads per space meant more revenue—an amazingly simple and straightforward concept. Media buyers such as Mindshare understood the model and allocated more clients' digital ad spending to them.

Over the next few years Focus Media's stock soared despite emerging questions about the advertising efficiency. The company grew through acquisitions, buying market research firm iResearch and Allyes, an online advertising firm. Tens of thousands of its digital screens popped up all over the country—along roadsides, near elevator banks, and in movie theaters.

Just as I warned Jiang, the screens broke earlier than expected. One in my office building did not work for months on end. Others became scratched, ruining the look of the advertisements. Later, one of Focus Media's senior executives admitted to me screens broke every two to three years and cost more to replace than imagined. Labor costs went up, too, so it was no longer cheap to send someone to upload content manually.

In 2011, Focus Media was blindsided by Muddy Waters, an investment research firm run by American Carson Block. Block published a scathing report accusing Focus Media of overstating the number of its screens by 50 percent. The company claimed Muddy Waters' allegations were exaggerated.

Block himself later faced accusations that he manipulated markets by colluding with hedge funds on reports, and has been proved wrong as much as right, but the damage had already been done. Investors abandoned Focus Media. Beset by a plummeting stock price, Jiang took his company private with the help of private equity (PE) firm FountainVest Partners. One of the partners at FountainVest told me just before its investment, "I think we can make money out of Focus Media by repositioning it."

Still, by that time Jiang had already banked his fortune.

In the late 1990s, none of China's fledgling tech start-ups—companies such as Sohu, Sina, and Focus Media—was known for being particularly innovative. They copied business models from Western players, such as Internet portal Yahoo! and JCDecaux, and tweaked them for Chinese consumers.

Nimble and market-oriented, these Chinese Internet players disrupted the dominance of stodgy old state-owned enterprises (SOEs) that were more concerned with catering to political masters than consumers.

Internet players delivered fresh content but used technology developed overseas. All day long, Sohu and Sina uploaded content on Chinese celebrities, food, and sports stars. Focus Media simply digitized advertising posters and moved faster than CCTV and other state-owned media outlets to offer different advertising media and packages to brands.

In those days there was so much money to make by copying proven business models from America that there was no real reason to be innovative. Charles Zhang, the founder of Sohu, exemplifies, too, an entrepreneur who became rich by copying what worked in America and tweaking it for China. He made hundreds of millions of dollars after his company's IPO in 2000, at a time when $60 a month was a decent salary.

Trying to be innovative probably would have hurt more than helped in raising capital and chanced creating too much *mafan,* or trouble, from conservative regulatory bodies, as one founder of a big Internet company told me in 2003. "Why take the risk," he said, when there were so many easy opportunities just to port over an existing model? You only needed to see the size of his houses or look at the number of companies, such as Bloomberg, that eventually conflicted with regulators, to realize he had a very good point.

Foreign investors in those days worried about being cheated. They had reason to be. Tales of Chinese companies duping gullible foreigners out of hundreds of millions of dollars abounded like urban legends, the type that would be famously recounted in books, such as Tim Clissold's 2004 book *Mr. China* and Paul Midler's *Poorly Made in China.* One due diligence project my firm, the China Market Research Group (CMR), did for a PE client highlights the risks well.

Our client wanted to buy a company that claimed it had 50 sales points throughout the country. The head of the PE firm even visited one sales point that was bustling and doing a resounding business. During our due diligence, we went to check out some of the other outlets—but could not find any. The Chinese firm had simply made them up and essentially built one fake outlet staffed with part-timers to show potential foreign investors.

To mitigate risk, some investors, such as Inter-Asia Venture Management, established in 1972 by Lewis Rutherfurd and Jim Hawes, put up half the capital to take Western companies to Asia instead of backing true Chinese start-ups. Inter-Asia would become the trusted local partner and then exit the investment through a trade sale back to the parent company.

Investors trusted Rutherfurd and Hawes. Rutherfurd came from a well-established blue-blooded family in America's Northeast. His grandfather was Frank L. Polk, a founding partner in the New York law firm Davis Polk & Wardwell. He had attended St. Paul's, Princeton, and then Harvard Business School, where he met Hawes, who had previously been a U.S. Navy Seal team instructor. Few Americans investing in China in those days had such gilded backgrounds as Rutherfurd and Hawes.

When I first met Hawes and Rutherfurd to join Inter-Asia's Shanghai office as chief of research and to be in charge of information technology (IT) investments, they were both around 60 and built like rocks. Rutherfurd led the entire Inter-Asia team on group hikes and runs, and Hawes still looked like he could go through a Navy Seal Hell Week with ease. Once we were on a ferry during a typhoon that to me seemed like it was about to capsize. Hawes calmly downed a full meal, guffawing while I squirmed and prayed to live another day.

Rutherfurd touted Inter-Asia's strategy of investing in Western brands' Chinese operations to potential investors as having "no business risk, just execution risk." Inter-Asia brought household names from the West, such as McDonald's and IKEA, to Asia and made millions. Pension funds and university endowments flocked to invest money into the firm's early funds. Regulators immediately saw the business model of McDonald's and other mature businesses and how they worked, and they were relatively quick to grant approvals.

By the late 1990s, foreign investors no longer remained content just to invest in the Chinese operations of Western companies. They wanted to localize investments and started backing home-grown Chinese start-ups, such as Sohu, Focus Media, and Sina. They also had a different exit strategy in mind—rather than Rutherfurd's strategy of relying mostly on trade sales, they wanted to exit through IPOs. Valuations for public listings were often much higher than what could be received from a trade sale to a corporation. Plus, public listings had the added benefit of catching the attention of the Western financial press, including the *Wall Street Journal,* which would write about their successes, making it easier to raise the next funds, and the cycle would begin again.

Investors remained scared about Chinese entrepreneurs cheating them, so they cautiously deployed capital. Instead of investing directly into Chinese firms, some firms, such as technology-focused venture capital firm Sutter Hill Ventures, put money into local venture capital firms run by Chinese investment professionals they trusted.

Sutter Hill, along with Yale's endowment, backed Chengwei Ventures, started by Eric Li, a Stanford graduate who later became famous for TED Talks and op-eds defending China's political system. Greylock Partners took a similar track to Sutter Hill by supporting Deng Feng's Northern Light Venture Capital instead of making direct investments on its own.

Other venture capital firms decided to take risks and open up shop in Shanghai and Beijing. Executives often had little in-country operating experience—and frequently didn't even have any Chinese-speaking employees aside from the secretary, driver, or junior analyst—but they still wanted a piece of the action. They tried to back mainland Chinese entrepreneurs who had returned to China from studying overseas (usually in the United States or the United Kingdom) and who spoke English well.

Due diligence often consisted of confirming the founder spoke good English, bathed regularly, and not much else. This is not an exaggeration: The China head for one of the world's most famous venture capital firms once rather condescendingly lamented to me that the entrepreneurs he met "all smell—they all smoke and go whoring at KTV (a kind of karaoke where men hire women to accompany them) bars. I don't know how to talk to them. Do you know someone who speaks English well and washes regularly?" and said if I did know someone, would I please introduce him.

Because of their uneasiness about operating in China and linguistic limitations, Western investors preferred simple, easy-to-understand business models that Western-educated Chinese ran. Baidu, the "Google of China," was founded by Robin Li, who had studied computer science at State University New York–Buffalo. Peggy Yu, a master of business administration grad of New York University's Stern School of Business set up online retailer Dang Dang—the Amazon of China. Jack Ma, who although not overseas educated had worked as an English teacher and could communicate easily with Westerners, positioned Alibaba's Taobao marketplace as the eBay of China. Renren, started by Joseph Chen, a University of Delaware and Stanford Business School alum, became the Facebook of China.

These copycat companies got capital investments from Western funds (Renren raised money from General Atlantic) or companies (Yahoo! invested $1 billion in Alibaba). At the time, China was still so poor and the market so immature that there were no meaningful Chinese venture capital firms, so entrepreneurs had to rely on foreign investors.

It became a joke that whenever a Silicon Valley tech start-up got funding, hundreds of copycat Chinese companies would start up within hours. It worked out well for a lot of them as well. Over the years founder after founder of these Internet copycats became wealthy without their companies ever having turned a profit.

Peggy Yu's Dang Dang took 11 years before it posted a single cash flow–positive quarter, and yet she had already become a billionaire by then from the company's 2010 IPO. Sina's Twitter-like microblogging platform, Sina Weibo, went public in April 2014 at a multibillion-dollar valuation, despite losing $47.6 million the quarter before. E-commerce retailer Mecox Lane raised $129 million and then saw its shares rally 57 percent on the first day after it went public in 2010 despite being unprofitable with a zero price/earnings (P/E) ratio.

Hedge fund and mutual fund investors forgave entrepreneurs for their lack of profits. Just as in the heady days of the Silicon Valley dot-com boom in the late 1990s, investors drooled at China's potential. They made investment decisions based on market share and sales growth, with little if any attention paid to return on equity or profits. Dang Dang's chief financial officer even explicitly announced after its IPO that it focused on market share and on increasing revenues because investors did not care about profits.

All the fervor from the international investment community taught China's tech entrepreneurs that trying to be innovative or care about profits did not make sense—as long as revenue and market share kept growing, they would personally get filthy rich, the bottom line be damned.

⟨≈⟩

Jason Jiang, like many Chinese entrepreneurs in the late 1990s and early 2000s, made money by creating a company with a business model Westerners could understand easily. He did not become rich through pioneering new technologies—he didn't need to. Rather, Jiang built his fortune by creating scale and market share.

Others, such as Charles Zhang at Sohu, were even more obvious, copying Western business models from Yahoo! and other American Internet players, but it did not matter—they got rich and gained respect internationally for their business prowess. The first time I saw Zhang was at an invite-only reception JP Morgan arranged to bring their international board to. Tony Blair, my wife, and I were talking about Chinese youth; I could see Zhang cornering Henry Kissinger.

Other entrepreneurs saw the success of Zhang and Jiang and realized there was no need to spend money on research and development. Jiang did not even try to automate the updating of the digital screens; it was more cost-effective to send low-paid employees to update the screens by hand.

Investors also hesitated to back innovative companies in those days. They made money backing copycats, such as Dang Dang, and straightforward concepts, such as Focus Media, so they spent little time looking for innovative companies. Everyone got rich in the process.

In the winter of 2014 I wanted to find out what the financiers thought of investing in innovation a decade earlier, when Charles Zhang and Jason Jiang were just starting their companies, and where innovation was now in China, so I arranged to have lunch with Rob McCormack, the founding partner of Shanghai-based Mustang Ventures.

A Stanford alumnus, McCormack had worked for leading venture capital firm Kleiner Perkins Caufield Byers in Silicon Valley in its heyday before starting his own China-focused firm. Few investors have such deep experience both in China and America in early stage investing.

McCormack invited me to a bustling vegetarian restaurant just behind Plaza 66 in Shanghai. We met at 11:30 to make sure we got a table before the lunchtime stampede from the nearby office towers. Tall and thin, McCormack wore preppie clothing—an Oxford shirt and khaki pants. With his height and confidence when speaking, he posed a towering presence even when seated.

As a server presented a dish of vegetarian-friendly ersatz chicken, McCormack started telling me about his investment strategy. He remained bullish about the health care sector and expected returns for early-stage ventures, which had been lower than later-stage and buyout funds, improving gradually in the coming years as the market matured.

We moved our discussion toward the state of innovation in the early days of the Chinese Internet era. As McCormack took a bite of food, I edged in a question about why there was seemingly so little innovation then.

McCormack told me that historically there had been "business model innovation, but not technological innovation." He differentiated innovation into two parts: (1) business model innovation, which Chinese firms were adept at, was taking technology from other countries and using it in a way specific for China and (2) technological innovation, which was more like invention.

The initial emphasis on business model innovation was natural, McCormack explained, because there were great opportunities to improve on business models from other countries and localize them for the particular needs of the Chinese market. This was similar to what Japan and South Korea had done at similar stages in their economies in the 1960s to 1990s. Even America had gone through a similar progression from copycatting European technology until the late nineteenth century, when America became innovative in its own right.

That made sense, I thought. There was so much low-hanging fruit during the 1990s that there was no need to invest in technological innovation. When Samsung and Sony were just starting, they also relied on making cheap copycat products. It was only once they became established global players that they started investing in innovation to improve margins and defeat market leaders at the premium level.

I thought about how to apply McCormack's theories to Jason Jiang at Focus Media. Jiang had not invented anything from a technological sense but had combined digital screens and advertising to come up with Focus Media. He was not technologically innovative but it was business model innovation to use these technologies to localize for the Chinese market specifically.

The server brought over some watered-down tea. After taking a sip, McCormack called the server over to double-check we had been served tea and not water by mistake and then continued, "Chinese entrepreneurs aren't stupid. They know the goal is to generate profits. It was too risky to invest in technological innovation in those days." I thought about the high costs and low success rates of true technological innovation for the companies that have attempted it in China's Internet space. I could not think of any successful examples of technological innovation between 2000 and 2005. Most had just copycatted Western models and made piles of dough.

For McCormack the lack of continued technological innovation essentially boiled down to the abundance of easy opportunities that still existed in what was still an immature and fast-growing market—the so-called low-hanging fruit. Over the past 15 years there simply has been too much money to make by tweaking ideas that worked elsewhere for the local market to spend too much money and energy on innovation. Why tax yourself reaching for branches higher up the tree when there are plenty of juicy apples hanging right in front of you?

The lack of innovation in China over the past 30 years clearly was the result of circumstances rather than some inherent inability within Chinese culture to innovate, as Panos Mourdoukoutas, a professor of economics at Long Island University Post in New York, argued in *Forbes* in 2012. He said Chinese cannot innovate because of what he calls "Confucian conformity," which stalls innovation and libertarian ideas.[1] In Mourdoukoutas's thinking, China can never be a hotbed of innovation, despite obvious historical inventions, such as gunpowder, multistage rockets, and the compass, as historian Joseph Needham pointed out in his series of books, *Science and Civilisation in China,* that took place when Confucianism was more embedded in society on a day-to-day basis than today.[2]

If historically China could innovate, it did not in recent decades for other reasons aside from a cultural inability—simply put, as the country reformed its economy starting in 1978 to allow for private enterprise, there was no need to invest in innovation. Lack of creativity in the education system or regulatory issues play a role undoubtedly in slowing innovation, but the natural evolution in the economy plays an even bigger role.

⸻

These days the lower branches are becoming sparser as more of the easy opportunities and quick turnarounds are plucked from the tree, and as we move closer to the 2020s, there will be still fewer easy opportunities.

Unlike a decade ago when the Chinese economy was so small it was an afterthought for most businesses, it has now become one of the key markets to win for multinationals. Companies will have to innovate more to offset increased competition from Chinese and international firms and higher input costs.

The pure copycat business model era that gave rise to Dang Dang and Sohu is over. Consumers no longer just want products copied from the West and tweaked a bit for local tastes—but ones developed with China in mind from the very beginning. In research my firm, CMR, has conducted with consumers throughout the country, we found that rising pride in the made-in-China label means consumers want to buy products made for China. When I started CMR in 2005, consumers were looking to what was popular in America and western Europe in fashion and technology to develop their identity. Our research in 2014 suggests consumers are now looking at trendsetters in China more so than ever before.

The change in opportunities for low-hanging fruit versus innovation mirrors the greater macroeconomic shifts in the Chinese economy. The economy, too, now is at a very different stage than when Jason Jiang started Focus Media. The 1990s and early 2000s were marked by the upheaval of Prime Minister Zhu Rongji's economic reforms of the late 1990s to transition from a socialist to a more market-oriented economy. Zhu forced SOEs to sell off assets—typically to well-connected individuals—and lay off tens of millions of workers in privatization and efficiency drives.

During this reordering of the economy, it was easy to make money if you were well connected and trusted by the leadership not to rock the political boat. One restaurant owner in a prime location in central Beijing told me while we were sitting in his multimillion-dollar mansion that he got a 20-year lease free from an SOE that owned the building "because they wanted to attract consumers to their development." Without rent costs his restaurant made $10 million in profits a year until 2013, when sales plummeted after the crackdown on government banquets and he had to shutter his business. Another son of a senior official told me he'd been granted a monopoly on selling

Australian wine to a specific ministry in one district of Beijing and had banked millions.

The drivers of China's economy are changing. President Xi Jinping's far-reaching crackdown on corruption, which he started in 2013 after ascending to the presidency, is forcing companies to become market rather than connection-oriented. Under President Xi, the government has been arresting people for corruption, such as Zhou Yongkang, China's former security czar and member of the Standing Committee of the Politburo and Xu Caihou, the former vice chairman of the Central Military Commission and Politburo member. Song Lin, the chair of China Resources, a holding company for energy land and consumer holdings, was arrested for graft. Jiang Jemin, the minister in charge of state-owned assets, also was sacked.

President Xi has changed procurement processes to make them more transparent and has limited how much and when officials can spend on dining, airplane tickets, hotels, and cars. Official banquets are now limited to "four dishes and one soup."

Companies that were based on patronage are shutting down while companies that can adjust to the new more transparent realities are thriving. Take, for instance, the high-end food sector in Beijing. Chef Da Dong's Roast Duck, a fancy peking duck chain, is posting record revenues and opening new outlets because it sells mostly to individuals rather than to government banquets or SOEs, whereas thousands of restaurants that relied on government patronage have faced losses or shut their doors entirely.

Overall the economy, too, is slowing as it moves away from overreliance on cheap credit and heavy investment to pump growth. Prime Minister Li Keqiang has set a 7.5 percent growth rate target for 2014 and wants to focus on sustainable growth rather than the growth-at-all-costs model of the previous decades. The government is now encouraging less pollution and return on equity in investments rather than pure gross domestic product (GDP) growth numbers.

Credit is tightening and the growth of the overall money supply has decelerated, slowing to only 12.4 percent in March 2014 from around 20 percent in previous years. There are fewer opportunities to make money simply by knowing the right people or doing large-scale heavy investment projects fueled by cheap credit.

The result of the more difficult macroeconomic environment, the crackdown on corruption, and demanding consumers is that more companies must move up the value stream and focus on innovation and branding or face squeezed margins or even bankruptcy. Copycatting business models won't cut it anymore in many sectors. Companies need to focus on both business model and technological innovation to maintain a long-term edge.

One of the great debates is even if entrepreneurs and financiers recognize the need for innovation, can it actually happen in China, or are there barriers (aside from Panos Mourdoukoutas's cultural inability argument)?

U.S. Vice President Joe Biden does not think China can innovate. He dared cadets at the Air Force Academy graduation on May 28, 2014, "I challenge you, name me one innovative project, one innovative change, one innovative product that has come out of China."[3] Stephen L. Sass, a professor emeritus from Cornell University in materials science and engineering, has similar arguments as Biden. He wrote in the *New York Times* in January 2014 that China cannot become innovative "until it moves its institutional culture away from suppression of dissent and toward freedom of expression and encouragement of critical thought."[4]

Is this really true? I thought to myself as I read Biden's and Sass's arguments. To see if their arguments had merit, I went out to interview entrepreneurs and investors in different sectors to see whether they embraced a shift toward innovation and what the remaining barriers were, specifically for examples of innovation in China.

The answer was clear, as we shall see: Biden and Sass are wrong—there is innovation taking place in China today, and there will be even more tomorrow because the seeds of innovation are being planted today. It would be a mistake for governments and companies to underestimate the ability of Chinese firms to move up the value chain because the barriers that have impeded innovation in China are slowly going away.

Chapters 2 and 3 will look at innovation and trends in the Internet, industrial, biotechnology, and health care sectors. Chapter 4 will look at the continued constraints and challenges facing innovation and potential for innovation in the next five years. It is clear China is already well along the way toward stage 2 on the innovation curve.

2

THE INNOVATION
CURVE STAGE 2
EMERGING INNOVATION

In 2004 I met an unassuming, thin Chinese man named Gary Wang for dinner along with a few friends on Hengshan Road in Shanghai. At first, Wang seemed to be the least charismatic of the group. He wore dark clothes, mumbled he did something with paper, and was relatively quiet as we talked about the differences between living overseas and in China.

We started talking about potential opportunities for starting or investing in companies. Wang came alive at the talk of entrepreneurship—he seemed to sit straighter in his chair and his eyes started to sparkle.

Underneath his unassuming exterior I could sense a drive and penetrating intelligence. As we walked to get after-dinner drinks, I asked if he wanted to remain in the paper business or switch to something else.

Wang looked me in the eyes and said, "I'm thinking about opening an online video site." I was overseeing information technology (IT) investments for Inter-Asia at the time, so his idea piqued my interest. I prodded him to explain more.

"I have a friend, a foreigner—we're thinking about doing something with sharing online videos," Wang said. The technology behind online video streaming was just starting to go mainstream, and he was figuring out how to harness the new technology to create a profitable business. No one in China, America, or anywhere else had been able to do it yet.

Wang's ideas remained at a very preliminary stage. He wasn't yet able to articulate exactly what he wanted to do or what his revenue model would be. YouTube, the online video sharing website Google eventually bought, had not yet launched. Hardly anyone used smartphones, most mobile phones still did not have touch screen technology, and what phones did have built-in cameras were far better at taking grainy still photos than video of any kind. Two words flashed like a warning sign in my head as Wang shared his ideas: *regulatory risk.*

I asked him about Chinese regulatory bodies, such as the State Administration of Press, Publication, Radio, Film and Television (SARFT), and how he would manage the risk of being banned and ensure that his company adhered to all relevant laws. On top of that there was also the risk that state-owned media giants, such as CCTV, would want to protect their virtual oligopolies on content and lobby the government to prevent new entrants from competing with them in the online sphere.

It was far from given that regulators would be hands-off about online video—indeed, even 10 years later in 2014, SARFT would force Sohu to stop streaming *The Big Bang Theory* and other popular Hollywood TV shows, such as *The Good Wife,* with an official editorial in a state-run newspaper citing the shows' "lewd and pornographic content." Sohu's stock tumbled, and meanwhile CCTV continued to air the far more licentious and violent HBO program *Game of Thrones* without incident.

Wang and I deliberated ways to surmount regulatory and commercial risk. I couldn't think of cost-effective measures. I suggested he hire waves of in-house employees to vet each uploaded video to ensure they followed laws and spend as much as needed to assure regulators they would be in full compliance. Or maybe he could hire or collaborate with the relation of a well-connected government official who could smooth regulatory issues away. Even then, there would still be no guarantees.

Wang didn't ask me for funding that night, because he was still in the initial stages of planning. Truth be told, I probably wouldn't have invested then—I worried not just about regulatory and commercial risk but also about the high cost of bandwidth and lack of a clear revenue model.

I didn't talk to Wang for several years. He eventually turned his ideas into Tudou, an online video sharing website whose name means simply *potato,* along with his partner Marc van der Chijs, a Dutch-born businessman living in Shanghai. I later met van der Chijs in 2007 in Shanghai and respected his acumen as I got to know him better—he also had that drive and sparkle Wang had.

In 2005, Wang and van der Chijs raised $500,000 in a seed round of funding. The next year they took in $8.5 million from venture capital firms IDG Ventures, Granite Global Ventures (GGV), and Jafco Ventures. Finally in 2007 and 2010 they added funding from General Catalyst Partners and the Singaporean sovereign wealth fund Temasek, raising more than $100 million all told.

When I spoke to van der Chijs in 2014, he attributed Tudou's success in funding to his and Gary's relative maturity—both were in their early 30s and had worked in multinationals and start-ups, whereas a lot of their competition was essentially straight out of college. "From the beginning we had a long-term vision and we were very clear in our talks to venture capitalists about this, while many of our competitors seemed to be more focused on quick money," he said. As he put it, their vision was to "create a platform for everybody to share their talents and become a star."

Van der Chijs says serious thought went into whether to make Tudou a worldwide website or a China-focused one. After long discussions they settled on focusing on mainland China specifically. "I believe that was the right decision," he said. "Only because of that focus could we make the online video site that Chinese wanted to go to and with content specifically for mainland China."

The decision paid off. Tudou quickly became vibrant when Internet access in China was growing by leaps and bounds (the Internet user base had ballooned from 13 million people in 2000 to 110 million in 2005 and increased by *64 million users a year* on average over the next seven years). The website became known for its user-created videos displaying the talents and creativity of everyday people in China. This was somewhat in contrast to YouTube, which in its early days, before copyright holders started defending their properties more aggressively, had a higher ratio of clips ripped from TV shows, such as *The Daily Show*, and proportionately less user-generated content.

Tudou especially became associated with *egao*—irreverent, user-created spoof videos making light of everyday topics in Chinese life—something that would never fly on staid mainstream networks, such as CCTV. The videos delighted Chinese Internet users, who were tired of watching sanitized, derivative soap operas on TV and craved fresh, creative content. To stoke creativity, Wang and van der Chijs started the Tudou Video Festival. "The original idea was to create a sort of Woodstock for independent

Chinese films," said van der Chijs, "but it grew into one of the biggest film festivals in China."

They don't get enough credit, but Wang and van der Chijs—not YouTube's Chad Hurley and Steve Chen—made online video sharing mainstream first. Tudou eventually went public in 2011 before rival video website Youku acquired it a year later in a $1 billion stock swap.

Wang has gone on to start an animation studio called Light Chaser Animation Studios and is attempting to revolutionize China's cartoon industry. The demand for indigenous creativity and entertainment is a hot topic; many investors who backed Tudou have followed Wang and furnished support for his new venture. After Tudou, van der Chijs ran online gaming and fashion retail start-ups in Shanghai before relocating to Vancouver in 2013 to take a partnership in the venture capital firm Cross-Pacific Capital, where he is banking on Bitcoin's rise.

Tudou's success heralded a new era among entrepreneurs. They realized that they didn't have to copy and adapt existing business models and that doing something that had not been done before could make them rich, too. More investors were willing to back start-ups, and Tudou's success made investors more comfortable backing companies with newer and potentially pathbreaking concepts. Investors such as Jenny Lee at GGV (see the Big Interview at the end of this chapter) started to take larger risks on companies such as multimedia social hangout YY and Internet dating app Momo—and were succeeding. Investors saw Lee's success and realized they no longer had to go just for easy wins.

Private equity investors now tout their prowess at backing innovation when raising money from limited partners (LPs), such as endowments, wealthy individuals, and pension funds. One executive at a multibillion-dollar private equity firm told me in 2014 that its strategy is to see how they can invest in Internet companies "that disrupt traditional industries." Terms such as *disruption* and *innovation* were not part of the lexicon 10 years ago, but they have now become mainstays in fund-raising proposals to investors.

Some companies still tout themselves as the Chinese version of some American company in their elevator pitch, like the Groupon or Square of China, but investors now are willing to hear about new business models as well. Few copycats get anywhere profit-wise anymore—most go bankrupt or are acquired on the cheap.

Seeing the riches born from innovation and looking for ways to stave off competition, mainstream Internet companies that started as copycats, such as Baidu, have also begun to innovate—even as they continue to grab low-hanging fruit—changing the intellectual landscape in China along the way.

I met Kaiser Kuo nearly a decade ago. At the time, the garrulous, long-haired Chinese American was the China bureau chief for Red Herring, a tech-focused media website, but he'd had a long and varied career in China from the 1990s onward, including as a founding member of the popular Chinese heavy metal band Tang Dynasty. One of his current side projects is hosting the China-focused Sinica Podcast. He also made international headlines in 2011, when Jeremy Goldkorn reported in *TechCrunch* that Kuo said Groupon was "getting it in the ass" in China.[1]

After working at Red Herring, Kaiser had stints at Ogilvy & Mather's digital practice and advised Youku, the online video company that acquired van der Chijs and Wang's Tudou. He now works as the director of international communications for Baidu—one of the early dominant Internet players that had been dubbed the Google of China for its popular Chinese-language search engine.

In his post at Baidu, Kuo is as well positioned as anyone to see the evolution of China's Internet players. I asked him why innovation had been limited in China in the recent past. For him it came down to necessity.

"All that low-hanging fruit [in the past] made it simply irrational for either entrepreneurs or their financial backers to go reaching into higher branches," he said. "It wasn't just a matter of being expensive and time-consuming; there was substantial consumer need for localized versions of other products."

Kuo's answer echoed what I'd heard from Rob McCormack of Mustang Ventures. In the early days of China's Internet, there was simply no need to innovate. Consumers were relatively undemanding. Just about anything a market-oriented private company offered trumped the offerings from lethargic state-owned enterprises (SOEs). Baidu's founder, Robin Li, topped China's list of rich people for several years, proving his initial model of copycatting Google was right.

As time went on and more and more Chinese gained a taste of overseas experience, whether through studying or traveling, their demands increased. Direct knockoffs or slight adaptations of foreign concepts became less interesting; an increasingly sophisticated user base began to demand not only best-of-breed products and services designed for the Chinese market specifically but also ones that were themselves innovative. "An increasingly large portion of the brand value of an Internet company is now related to innovation," Kuo told me. "Chinese Internet companies now really need to sell the idea that they're capable of 'real'—not just incremental—innovation. It's now part of the culture."

To hold on to its dominant market position, Baidu has been launching and updating innovative products beyond its basic Google-like search app, such as Baidu Translate and Baidu Maps, and has been constantly adding new services within these tools. It also bought innovative companies, including the mobile app store 91 Wireless for $1.9 billion in 2014.

In May 2014, Baidu made even greater steps when it hired Andrew Ng, who headed Stanford University's artificial intelligence head lab and announced he would lead a $300 million 200-researcher research and development center built in Silicon Valley. Baidu is no longer content to copycat Google—it has branched off and focused on innovation to fill consumers' needs before they even realize they have those needs.

But Baidu has not shifted completely into investing in innovative products only, said Kuo. "There's some impressive stuff, but the truth is there's still a goodly amount of low-hanging fruit." Kuo sees the key opportunities in tech as a balance between both genuine innovation as well as the easier wins that still exist in the market. "Investment capital is still going to flow toward areas where returns are more likely, and it's a safe bet that more 'copy to China' is in the cards in the next few years at least. But I have absolutely no doubt that this is already changing [toward more innovation], and barring any catastrophe will only accelerate in coming years."

❦

"He's small. I mean, *really* small," the American Internet tech legend squawked, demonstrating a thinly spaced thumb and index finger. It was 2006, and she had just been to Hangzhou to meet Jack Ma, the founder of Alibaba. "He's much shorter than I expected."

That was all that Internet legend had to say about Ma. Whether she dismissed him because of his diminutive stature or for some other reason, five years later Ma's Alibaba had trounced that American Internet company in China. The American company had spent tens of millions trying to get into China with little luck and today is a shell there, occupying a negligible sliver of the market yet remaining a household name in America.

Jack Ma, whose Chinese name is Ma Yun, may be small in stature, but his influence on China's economy over the past 15 years cannot be overestimated. Business circles regard him as tough as nails. One influential businessperson told me, "He's so ruthless, driven and arrogant that I'll never work with him" but conceded grudgingly that Ma is "damn good at what he does." Despite—or perhaps because of—his cold-blooded demeanor, Ma has shaken up his country's economy and traditional industries more than all but a handful other entrepreneurs. Thinking of people who have had a comparable impact in the United States, Bill Gates, Henry Ford, Steve Jobs, and not very many others come to mind.

Ma's company, Alibaba, dominates the world's largest e-commerce market today. Now he is disrupting the status quo further by branching into private wealth products, banking, professional soccer, and a host of sectors long dominated by inefficient SOEs.

Breaking down barriers is something Ma is used to doing. First he used the Internet to create a business-to-business platform to make the process of sourcing products easier, more transparent, and trustworthy. At a time when sourcing from China was taking off, Ma gave small companies around the world the ability to do so without hiring expensive intermediaries or spending lots of money on travel expenses. At this stage Alibaba was copycatting business models or, arguably, doing business model innovation rather than technological innovation.

He then built Taobao to transform how individuals and small mom-and-pop stores sold their wares, trouncing eBay in the process. The huge range of products available on Taobao was a boon to consumers throughout China but especially to those in lower-tier cities, whose shopping choices until then had been limited by the relatively slow rollouts of brick-and-mortar store chains beyond the larger cities.

Reviews of sellers and buyers reduced the risk of being cheated by unsavory businesspeople who sold copies and fakes of products. Crucially, Alibaba's Alipay system—which, unlike foreign services such as PayPal, held customers' payments in escrow until they could confirm receipt of the products they had bought—surmounted a key barrier to shopping online for Chinese consumers, who were wary of unscrupulous vendors sending them fake or faulty goods. This improvement filled a void left by state-owned banks, such as Bank of China and Industrial and Commercial Bank of China (ICBC), which should have offered such a service but failed to because they were so focused on servicing SOEs.

Taobao and Ma have come under criticism for allegedly enabling the sales of counterfeit goods as many small shops open, shutting only once copyright holders find them out. Brands often accuse Alibaba of moving too slowly to police its website or of turning a blind eye. But with the amount of money and consumer trust at stake, Alibaba has begun policing Taobao websites to get rid of counterfeits. It spends more than $16 million a year fighting fake goods. In 2013 it removed more than 100 million listings it thought were infringing on copyrights. The efforts have been too little and ineffective, according to critics, because there are more than 7 million vendors selling 800 million items.

To combat counterfeiting, Alibaba launched Tmall, which sold products directly from online storefronts operated by the brands themselves. Adidas and Burberry were among key brands to open Tmall stores, which helped build credibility and assure consumers that Tmall was a place to buy genuine articles. Although Taobao offered breadth and cheaper prices, consumers flocked to Tmall because of its trustworthiness. Tmall's success has disrupted the department store and self-branded website models in the process. One senior Adidas executive told me, "We sell far more products on Tmall than through our own branded website and expect to allocate more efforts there going forward."

Tmall, because it signed deals with brands directly, has become one of the most trusted sales channels in the country despite Taobao's somewhat dodgy reputation. Consumers often trust Tmall more than brick-and-mortar stores that they fear sell fake or expired products. Alibaba has beaten Western players, such as eBay and Amazon, because it understands the needs of consumers and caters to them. For instance, after acquiring Chinese Internet player Eachnet (itself a copycat of eBay), rebranding it as eBay, eBay executives changed the user interface from the cluttered one that Eachnet originally used and Chinese consumers like, to a crisp, clean one popular in America. It also changed its hosting to America from China despite the protests of local executives, which made access speeds slower. Combined, eBay quickly lost its dominant position to Alibaba and eventually retreated from the market completely.

Ma's early initiatives often focused on business model innovation and tweaking existing concepts, such as eBay, PayPal, and Amazon.com, rather than true innovation. The model worked and Ma has become a multibillionaire. He and cofounder Joseph Tsai got so wealthy that they set up a $3 billion philanthropic trust, China's largest by far in 2014. But threats to Alibaba's dominance emerged that caused Ma to focus more on developing business lines that were wholly new.

After exploding in size throughout the 2000s, China's online population began shifting to their phones. The number of mobile Internet users grew from 143 million in 2010 to 510 million in early 2014, nearly all of them smartphone users. Many mobile phone users, many of whom are migrant workers who move from city to city and are price sensitive, refuse to sign long-term mobile phone contracts. They prefer to buy pay-as-you-go top-up cards and use Wi-Fi rather than data plans.

In 2011 Tencent, a Shenzhen-based company that had made most of its money through online games, advertising, and its instant messaging platform QQ, launched its blockbuster mobile communication app WeChat. WeChat was often compared to WhatsApp initially, and although it did have superficial similarities, it added a far more robust array of features, making it much closer to a Facebook-style social networking platform. "WeChat is based on chat apps like WhatsApp, but it used innovation to become a much more useful product," said van der Chijs. Like WhatsApp, it automatically suggested friends to connect to based on the phone numbers already saved on the user's contact list, and like Facebook it gave users a space to post personal updates, photos, songs, and videos to share with friends.

But a few key differences in functionality set it apart: First, the inclusion of short recorded voice memos filled an unmet need for quick communication in Chinese, a language whose tones and large number of homophones have impeded the development of speech-to-text dictation; second, keeping both status updates and comments and likes from friends visible only to people who are connected to each other made for a more private, intimate social network that Chinese users felt safer about using. It also incorporated a scanner for two-dimensional quick response (QR) codes, which people used for adding friends, joining chat groups, getting coupons, tracing the origins of produce in grocery stores, and many other uses.

WeChat quickly gained traction. Within just three years of existence, WeChat has already surpassed 300 million users and taken market share in countries such as India, Indonesia, and Brazil. I cannot even remember the last time someone in China asked for my e-mail or phone number—everyone asks for my WeChat ID.

Van der Chijs sees WeChat as an example of the Chinese style of innovation by necessity. "What you see is that Chinese companies often copy a concept that is successful in the Western world, but then make it much better than the original concept. So they innovate existing successful concepts. The main reason for this is that there is so much competition in China that you can't just copy a concept; you have to differentiate yourself in order to win. So you are forced to innovate; otherwise other companies will take over your market."

The rise of WeChat has disrupted several sectors at once, in the same way Alibaba did. Tencent's free communication tools hurt the profitability of mobile telecom carriers, such as China Mobile and China Unicom, as consumers stopped sending traditional short message service (SMS) text messages and even making voice calls, preferring instead to use WeChat's text chats and voice memos. Users of Sina's Twitter-like Weibo service suddenly shifted to using WeChat instead because it was easier to use on smartphones and safer because only people they specified could see their updates.

Tencent didn't stop at shaking up the telecom and social media worlds. Because WeChat was so popular, in many ways it took over users' whole mobile phone interface, adopting more and more functions, such as maps and videoconferencing, and eliminating the need for other apps. Users turned on their phones and went straight to WeChat to chat with friends, read their posts, and install apps within WeChat, effectively making it an alternate operating system. Tencent started to roll out ways to make purchases through WeChat's payment system and QR code scanner, both online and in physical stores.

Until the emergence of WeChat, Alibaba had dominated the Internet e-commerce space. But by colonizing more and more parts of consumers' smartphone interface, Tencent started to chip away at Alibaba's dominance. Tencent started to buy stakes in other companies, including JD.com, the country's largest online retailer after Tmall (see the interview in Chapter 7 with Richard Liu, the founder of JD.com). It also bought stakes in Dianping, a restaurant review site, as well as the taxi-hailing service Didi Dache.

By integrating payment systems into WeChat, Tencent started to compete with Alibaba's dominance for payment systems and e-commerce, too. By early 2014, 20 to 30 percent of all e-commerce sales were done through the mobile phone, so the threat Tencent posed to Alibaba was serious. That was a huge increase from just a year before, when it was only 5 to 10 percent. In winter 2013, the China Market Research Group (CMR) did research into consumers' usage habits of WeChat for a hedge fund. We found consumers said they mainly still browsed on mobile phones and bought on home computers. They were nervous to buy products via WeChat, but that changed by the end of 2013 as Tencent pushed mobile e-commerce and built trust with consumers.

Consumers could even buy wealth management products and send red envelopes of lucky money to friends via WeChat. By integrating with e-commerce sites, WeChat threatened Taobao's and Tmall's business models because consumers could bypass them to go directly to JD.com and other websites but still have a convenient way to pay for products.

With a looming initial public offering in 2014 on the horizon, Ma had to gain more control of the mobile phone space, so he started to acquire stakes in—or entirely buy out—mobile companies. Alibaba bought AutoNavi Holdings, a digital mapping and navigation firm, in a deal valuing the company at $1.5 billion. It took a 33 percent stake in Sina Weibo as well as a $1.22 billion stake in Youku.

Tencent and Alibaba seemingly made acquisitions daily to get an edge. Both invested in taxi-ordering services. For entrepreneurs, developing innovative products in the mobile space to sell their companies to Tencent or Alibaba paid off because they could command higher valuations than even by taking companies public.

Not content to just battle other Internet players, Ma also entered the ring to battle state-owned companies in the closed-off but lucrative financial sector. He launched wealth management products, offering higher interest rates than the banks' meager cash deposit services. Ma's rates were so high that depositors started taking money out of banks, helping precipitate an interest rate crunch in January 2014. Banks started to worry about meeting minimum capital reserves, sending interbank lending rates soaring.

Ma almost single-handedly forced state-owned banks to change interest rate policies and get interest rate reform on the table. State-owned banks fought back, trying to get regulators to stop online transfers to Alibaba and Tencent's wealth management products. Banks started limiting how much could be wired out and started to push regulators to worry about the security of the Internet giant's payment systems. Ma lashed out at the banks on Alibaba's messaging app Laiwang, "Let the users decide who wins the game, not monopoly and power. The market is not scared of competition. But it does fear injustice."

But the battle, at least in the minds of consumers, was clearly won by Alibaba and Tencent. Already disliking the service of state-owned banks, consumers rallied to support Alibaba by continuing to use and buy its services. As one consumer, a 28-year-old woman from Beijing, told me, "Alibaba and Tencent are more user-friendly and have better products than the state-owned banks."

Instead of blocking progress, to their credit, regulators have allowed the debate to continue and allowed the Internet players to encroach on the banks' domain to create competition and force the state-owned banks to reform.

To reduce banking crisis risks, and prevent the shadow banking sector, nonbank financial intermediaries that provide similar services as traditional banks offer and could include hedge funds and money market mutual funds (and not just guys in back alleys with bats loaning out money, as many seem to think), from expanding dangerously, banks must reform and rein in excess credit. They have often resisted central-government orders to reform in the past. China's central bank, the People's Bank of China, allowed the overnight interbank lending rate to soar in summer 2013 and cause a minor panic—it was an attempt to force banks to reform.

With nimble, innovative private players Alibaba and Tencent competing for retail clients, banks can no longer rely so much on the state and need to be more market-oriented. The head of one of the largest state-owned banks perfectly summed up the previous prevailing mentality to me in 2007, remarking, "I care about getting credit to SOEs—I don't care about retail customers. I get promoted based on making state-owned enterprises happy, not on profits."

Another executive committee member of a big state-owned bank said to me in 2011, "How much we loan out really doesn't matter; the government will always bail us out." The implicit backing of the government allows banks to follow unsustainable business practices and creates a moral hazard.

Consumers are unhappy with the current banking system. In interviews my company conducted with 1,000 consumers in first- and second-tier cities, more than 90 percent reported being dissatisfied or very dissatisfied with Bank of China. The number was slightly better for ICBC at 86 percent.

Ma understood consumer dissatisfaction with the banks. He declared that the state-owned banks take care of only 20 percent of banking customers and that he simply wants to serve the other 80 percent.

Around 80 million Chinese have bought Alibaba's wealth management products online via Yu'E Bao in search of better returns by the end of the first quarter in 2014. Tencent's competitive product, Licaitong, sold more than 700 million renminbi ($111 million U.S.) of products by investors on its launch day in the same year.

Tencent's and Alibaba's innovations have also cut into the dominance of the state-owned telecom sector. Aside from consumers switching from texting to WeChatting, the government has forced China Mobile and other carriers to sell bandwidth to Alibaba and other private Internet players to spur reform. China Mobile has some of the world's most expensive data plans. In the new Shanghai free-trade zone, the government is allowing private companies with more than one million renminbi in registered capital to invest in the telecom sector.

Xi Jinping's government not only has allowed for innovation in the Internet finance and telecom sectors so far but has also actively promoted it. Some analysts, such as Stephen L. Sass, have argued that the government has stalled innovation through overregulation, but in Internet finance and telecom it has played a positive role most of the time while ensuring consumer safety.

Alibaba's and Tencent's successes at business model and true technological innovation have emboldened investors and entrepreneurs and delighted consumers. Although there is still low-hanging fruit in the market, the better capitalized and more vibrant Internet players are betting on innovation for a bigger and bigger share of their profits. They have to, or else they will fall behind large well-capitalized companies as they buy up innovative companies.

The historical lack of innovation in China is the natural result of economic development as the country moved from a state-dominated economy to one more attuned to market forces. The government previously often slowed innovation down to protect state industries or for political worries over instability but gradually has embraced financial and Internet innovation to push for economic reform. In 2006, the Chinese government declared its intention to transform China into an innovative society by 2020 and a world leader in science and technology by 2050. In its 2006 *National Medium- and Long-Term Plan for the Development of Science and Technology (2006–2020)* (MLP), it started to encourage innovation.

Too strong a regulatory hand often makes entrepreneurs and financiers hesitate when deploying resources and often runs counter to the government's MLP. For instance, should companies such as Sohu pay for the rights to stream *The Big Bang Theory* legally if regulators might order them to take it down without much warning, or is it better to pirate Hollywood shows so that if one is hit by regulatory issues, the money lost is less? The government needs to increase transparency of regulations to encourage the risk taking necessary to create a culture of innovation.

⊰⊱

The IT space is not the only arena where Chinese companies have become competitive on a global scale. Industrial sectors, such as construction equipment, are hotbeds for innovation, too, and are no longer just transferring technology from America and Europe to China. Chinese construction equipment makers Sany and Xugong have taken market share from long dominant Western players, such as Terex and Caterpillar, by going global. Sany has opened factories in Georgia in America and acquired Putzmeister, a German company making high-tech concrete pumps. Also, Sany has hired foreign industrial designers.

One buyer of excavators told me, "We buy Sany products because they're *better* than foreign equipment makers—not because they're cheaper." Board members for Terex or Caterpillar should be concerned; to maintain edges, they have to invest in innovation, accept squeezed margins, or launch cheaper brands. Most likely a combination of all three will be necessary.

Industrial players relying on cheap labor have been forced to handle rising labor and real estate costs by moving up the value stream. No longer can they afford to compete with cheap but good-enough products. Unlike multinational players with diverse revenue streams, Chinese players had to react quickly to squeezed margins in their home market by focusing on brand building, innovation, and worker efficiency.

Senior executives at mobile phone carriers, such as Norway's Telenor and South Korea's SK Telecom, told me of the shift. They told me they bought Huawei's telecom equipment rather than Ericsson's because the "equipment was better quality." A senior executive at Cisco admitted in 2014, "Huawei is getting much better technologically. We are still better but the gap is narrowing. We have to keep spending on research and development to maintain our edge."

A Booz & Company innovation survey in 2013 found two-thirds of multinational company (MNC) respondents said some of their Chinese competitors "are already at least as innovative as their own companies."[2] The tide has shifted and Chinese companies are moving away from copying Western technology to focusing on innovation.

For Julian Cheng, a managing director with Warburg Pincus, one of the world's largest private equity firms, this shift is a natural progression. He told me, "Industries have to become mature enough before you start to innovate. It takes a decade of industrial formation." Cheng's analysis makes sense. Industrial firms mostly privatized in the late 1990s, so they have just reached the point where they can start thinking about innovation.

It takes years, not decades, to compete on innovation, much as it did for Japanese and Korean firms. But the gap is closing much faster than analysts such as Anne Stevenson-Yang, the founder of J Capital Research, think. Stevenson-Yang argued in 2014 in an online debate for the *Economist* that innovation in China has been "thwarted by government domination of the economy."[3]

Although regulatory issues or "government domination" might hamper innovation, they are not the biggest barriers—it would be a mistake to discount the innovation taking place in the private sector. Also, in many ways, the dominance of the state-owned sector, and its slowness in financial services and telecom, is precisely what gave Alibaba and Tencent the impetus to focus on innovation and deliver to the market something SOEs could not.

One autumn day I visited Mr. Zhu, one of 3M's most senior Chinese executives, to hear his views on innovation. Known as one of the most innovative companies in the world along with Google and Apple, 3M had been doing business in China since 1984 and generated 10 percent of its global revenue there in 2013. It built its largest research and development (R&D) center outside of America in China.

Zhu motioned to me to sit and gave me a cup of green tea. In the corner of his office quietly hummed of one of 3M's best-selling air purifiers.

I asked Zhu whether he thought Chinese industrial firms were becoming more innovative or whether they were they still growing by copying Western innovation and winning on sales and distribution.

Zhu reflected. "Technologically, foreign firms were historically far superior to the domestic Chinese firms," Zhu said, "but the gap is narrowing as the Chinese firms go up the value stream." Starting in 2012, he said, is when he started seeing 3M's Chinese competitors make great strides on the technology side.

He admitted, "3M's products are superior to Chinese firms—but not as much as before." The narrowing gap has affected some of 3M's business units because they have had to decrease margins to maintain an edge and had to invest more to maintain that lead. They have also had to innovate more in other sectors, such as air purification systems, to maintain their overall growth, margin, and profit targets.

I asked why Chinese firms were getting so competitive. Zhu pointed out that Chinese companies were now poaching executives from multinational firms, offering competitive pay and spending more money on R&D. He wrinkled his brow. "Some also think there is a 'bamboo ceiling' in place for Chinese in multinationals."

More resources being invested in Chinese firms and bamboo ceilings were issues I had heard of before. I'd seen many top-notch Chinese executives leave jobs with multinationals to work at Chinese firms because they felt they could not be promoted. They saw few mainlanders promoted to top echelons and thought headquarters did not trust locals.

In certain sectors that had government support, such as solar power and other forms of renewable energy, Chinese firms backed with low interest rates from banks were borrowing more money to focus on R&D than many Western firms that were still struggling from weak economies in their home markets. For many Chinese they simply had more resources and more personal power working for a Chinese company.

Zhu continued, "Foreign companies overall are still at the forefront but they need to continue to innovate to stay ahead of Chinese competition. Innovation is something 3M continues to focus on." He pointed to the air purifier in his office. He told me that new products, such as air and water purifiers, are bolstering 3M's revenue, which makes up for challenges in other divisions that are under more attack from domestic competition.

I asked him whether he was more worried about other multinational competitors or Chinese. "Chinese," he answered quickly, "because they're improving so much faster than their foreign counterparts."

3M remains one of the most innovative companies in the world, yet their senior executives, including Zhu, do not underestimate domestic competitors' ability to innovate. They understand markets change and to stay ahead of the curve, 3M needs to focus on innovation and not belittle competition.

Across sectors Chinese firms are becoming more innovative. Discounting the ability of Chinese firms to go up the value chain, as Vice President Biden does, would be a mistake because the improvements can come quickly. It would be better to heed the warnings of the executives at 3M.

Jenny Lee, Managing Partner of GGV in Shanghai

Originally a fighter jet upgrade engineer, Jenny Lee is one of China's most successful venture capitalists. A graduate of Cornell University with bachelor of science and master of engineering degrees, and a master of business administration degree from

Kellogg School of Management at Northwestern University, Lee did a 180-degree switch from tech to banking at Morgan Stanley. By the time I first met her in 2003, when she was at Jafco, she was already building a reputation as one of the top venture capitalists in Asia. Over the last decade her career has soared with GGV.

She invested in YY (NASDAQ: YY), of which she is a board member; 21Vianet Group (NASDAQ: VNET); Pact (NASDAQ: PACT); SinoSun Technology (listed in ChiNext); and UCWeb. While with GGV, she has taken a total of five companies between 2010 and 2012. She is also an angel investor in the Chinese smartphone maker Xiaomi. Her favorite quote to entrepreneurs: "If you can go for the *gold*, never settle for just *silver*."—in other words, aim for number one always: No one remembers the person who comes in second.

Rein: Can Chinese firms innovate or do they simply copycat Western companies like Google?

Lee: I am a big believer in Chinese innovation and this can be best showcased in business model innovation. Fifteen years ago when China's Internet was in its infancy, it was only natural that there be a need for a Chinese search engine, hence Baidu, a Chinese e-commerce site, hence Alibaba, but note before Google, there were Yahoo!, Excite, @home, and Lycos. The world of search through the Internet browser is a basic need, but the engine always needed to be localized for local sites, local usage, and so on.

Today, in an increasingly crowded Internet market, with 20 to 30-plus Chinese Internet companies with over $1 billion market capitalization and category leaders in search, commerce, social network, travel, portal already staked out, Chinese entrepreneurs now have to compete not by copying another company's business model but by innovating and adapting to local user needs and behavior.

Rein: Can you share examples of innovative Chinese companies?

Lee: Examples are Qihoo, YY (which I am on their board), and Xiaomi (I am an angel investor). YY showed the world that you can create a real-time communication network through their strong back-end technology by changing the way users play games and interact online, sing and entertain each other online as well as disrupting traditional education by empowering individuals to showcase their talent or skills (singing, teaching, etc.) online without the need to be tied to an institution. There is no model like YY in the world.

Xiaomi showed the world that a company can converge the best of hardware, software, and services to create a new-age fan-based mobile Internet platform company. Xiaomi not only disrupted the traditional phone makers' ecosystem from supply to distribution to retail but also showed what it means to bring the Internet DNA to the old world of phone makers. Extending that into home consumer electronics, like TV, tablets, XiaomiTV.

The word *innovation* is no longer just the domain of hardcore technology. It is the use of technology to create new business models that can create real value for the people. This is real-world innovation. Innovation without creating real dollar value is not innovation, just research.

Rein: What are the major constraints to innovation in China?

Lee: China is perfect for innovation because traditional revenue models (like charging advertising for revenue, etc.) is too simple, easily copied, and therefore low barriers to entry. The competitive Chinese environment forces companies to innovate in order to survive. The need for survival is the necessary ingredient for creating sparks of innovation and creativity in business models' innovation.

Today, the talent pool has increased tremendously and we are seeing quite a few serial entrepreneurs. There is also enough success in the 130-plus listed technology companies overseas to continue to create a supply of talents, both on the senior management level, middle-level managers, and engineers as they leave to do their own start-ups.

Regulation is a double-edged sword. On one hand, it gives local start-ups a window of opportunity to grow before foreign competitors enter. On the other hand, like in the case of online video sharing, having to apply for the right license or getting the necessary online video sharing permits can delay the growth of the business or put a company out of business. It can protect yet at the same time, weed out the smaller or weaker players.

I always like to say that if you can survive China's harsh, fiercely competitive Internet market, then you are ready for the world. Much like if you can survive the harsh pollution in Beijing, the rest of the world smells balmy.

Abolish Bamboo Ceilings

It amazes me how many Fortune 500 companies do not count a single mainland Chinese executive among their executive management teams in China. I met with the China executive committee of a Fortune 50 company in 2013—not a single mainlander was in the room. Later, I asked one of the executives, an American, why they did not have any mainlanders. He said, "We do have Chinese. We have plenty of executives from Taiwan and Hong Kong."

I asked him if the company had trouble retaining their top mainland Chinese talent. He said they did. *No wonder*, I thought.

He was genuinely surprised when I told him that mainland Chinese need to see other mainlanders in positions of authority or else they feel they have no way to move up the corporate ladder, because in his mind, Hong Kongers and mainlanders were interchangeable. In the human resource context, most mainlanders view Taiwanese and Hong Kong executives as foreigners and do not feel they have futures in companies without senior mainland executives.

The fight for talent remains a key battle for MNCs—and it will only get worse. In the late 1990s, young university graduates dreamed to work for multinationals, such as Motorola and Procter & Gamble (P&G). In 2014, CMR surveys found younger Chinese desired jobs with SOEs, which touted high benefits, such as low interest rates to buy homes, whereas experienced workers wanted to move to private Chinese firms, where there were more opportunities for career growth.

Key Action Items: Companies need to localize management teams and have at least one mainland Chinese executive at the top of the pecking order. That executive needs to be paid as well as—if not better than—foreign counterparts. Top-performing Chinese executives are no longer willing to be treated as second-class citizens.

Focus on Ingredient and Supply Chain Innovation

Fierce competition from domestic Chinese players moving up the value chain who excel at distribution means industrial companies need to focus on efficiency and environmental friendliness in production lines. Take for instance Almax Mannequins, established in Italy in 1969 by Saverio Catanese. Saverio's son, Massimiliano Catanese, is the CEO today and faced a competitive threat from Chinese players who compete on price and scale.

To stay ahead, Catanese and the Asian CEO for Almax, Pier Giraudi, invested millions to build a factory in Shanghai, employing innovative production processes, embedded digital technology made in conjunction with IBM into mannequins, and automated production lines.

Instead of making mannequins with traditional fiberglass, which take a lot of manual labor to make and are high polluting, Almax focused on improving efficiency of facilities and using innovative ingredients. In general, most Chinese factory workers are only one-quarter as productive as counterparts in America or Germany.

Almax uses innovative ingredients, such as polystyrene, that allow recycling of mannequins. Almax closed the production cycle to ensure zero waste—water is recycled and dust filtered out of the air, mission critical selling points to clients with environmentally friendly goals. Most mannequins made by Chinese brands that rely on fiberglass are not recyclable, so Almax's zero waste is a major differentiator.

Unlike most domestic Chinese competitors that rely on manual labor, Almax automated production lines. It can ship environmentally friendly mannequins faster than competitors can ship polluting ones and can ship more—critical with the advent of fast fashion where in-store displays constantly change to attract end consumer foot traffic.

Fashion retail brands, such as H&M from Sweden and Zara from Spain, launch new clothing lines every few weeks, rather than once a season, and thus need more mannequins with different postures to handle new designs and in-store displays. Companies don't want to throw mannequins into landfills. Almax has gained share because it can get product to the door faster than competitors and recycle old mannequins.

Key Action Item: To deal with rising labor costs and adhere to client demands for environmental friendliness, manufacturing companies need to improve worker efficiency and build zero-waste production lines. China will not lose its manufacturing dominance any time soon because it has the infrastructure in place, but the nature of its production will go higher value. Light industry that relies on manual labor must relocate to other countries, such as Cambodia, Thailand, and Sri Lanka.

3

THE INNOVATION CURVE STAGE 2 CONTINUED

INNOVATION FOR CHINA, BIOTECHNOLOGY, AND HEALTH CARE

I got lost driving to Dr. Shi Lei's office located in Zhangjiang Hi-Tech Park in Shanghai. The map on my GPS I had bought the year before was already outdated—many of the roads I was driving on and the buildings I was passing had gone up in the past 12 months.

I messaged Shi via WeChat, saying I was lost. He responded he would come down to meet me in a hotel parking lot next to his office. I eventually found it. As I got out of the car, I realized Shi was much taller than I had expected—about 6′1″ in a country where the average height for adult males is just less than 5′7″. He had his coat pulled tightly around him as rain started to fall in plump, muddy droplets of water mixed with air pollution particles.

Shi is the director of antibody research and head of the China operations for RuiYi, a biotechnology start-up Professor Raymond Stevens of the Scripps Institute founded in San Diego. I had set up an appointment with Shi to hear his ideas about innovation in the biotechnology sector in China.

Copyright infringement remained a problem in biotech and health care, just as in the Internet sector. Newspaper headlines always touted police raids on shipments of counterfeit medical products, such as Viagra and condoms. French customs at the port of Le Havre announced in February 2014 that they had seized 10 metric tons of counterfeit aspirin, erectile dysfunction pills, and antidiarrheal drugs stashed in two shipping containers declared as Chinese tea.

Was intellectual property theft and counterfeiting stopping innovation in biotech, I asked, or was heavy-handed regulation? After all, it can take years of research before discoveries can be monetized, so I wanted to know whether it was worth investing all that money and time if counterfeiters could just steal technology or if state-owned enterprises could box out private companies. I thought surely intellectual property concerns had to be a huge obstacle for developing a strong biotech industry—after all, most multinational companies kept their most advanced tech production outside of China because of fears of intellectual property theft. Within minutes of starting our conversation, Shi disabused me of my notions.

⬥

Shi's story starts 24 years before in 1990. Shi was a gangly, 21-year-old undergraduate enrolled at Shanghai's famed Fudan

University. Admittance into Fudan was seen as a ticket to job security with a plum position in a state-owned company or the government after graduation.

Despite the prestige and security of being at Fudan, Shi decided he had to leave in the middle of his studies to seek better education opportunities. It can be hard to imagine now, in a country bulging with towering skyscrapers, luxury shopping malls, and a 12 percent obesity rate, but in the late 1980s and early 1990s, the country's economic progress was not guaranteed. More than 50 percent of the country lived below the absolute poverty line as defined by the United Nations. Meat was still a rare luxury for most of the population, as were hot showers. Anxious for a better life, many top minds left the country.

Shi ended up finishing his undergraduate studies at the University of Illinois in Chicago, where he completed a BS and a PhD. He also received MSc and EMTM degrees from the University of Pennsylvania. Recruited by leading institutions in America after graduation, Shi conducted research on immunology, animal modeling, and infectious diseases at Harvard Medical School's Massachusetts General Hospital, the world's largest hospital-based biomedical research program, before moving to the corporate side at Johnson & Johnson to design and characterize artificial scaffold proteins.

Raising a family with his wife, a Beijing native who herself had a fast-rising career at chemical giant DuPont, Shi stayed in America for two decades and realized the American dream: a big home, a growing family, and career success. Yet despite all their accomplishments, Shi and his wife started to get the itch to move back to China.

Shi found his opportunity with RuiYi, a start-up backed by 5AM Ventures, Versant Ventures, Apposite Capital, Glaxo SmithKline's SR One, Aravis SA, and Merck Serono Ventures. It raised a $15 million B-round in March of 2014. RuiYi conducts pathbreaking research in molecular biology and biochemicals to discover drug leads using cell biology and has a pipeline of monoclonal antibodies to G protein–coupled receptors (GPCRs), which are used for therapeutic needs. Shi established the Chinese arm to conduct research to create injectable drugs to target hard-to-cure diseases, such as cancer.

Shi motioned to the vacant office complex next to his. His neighbor, another biotechnology company, had expanded so quickly that it had just relocated to a larger multistory building down the street. RuiYi was hiring more people, too, and adding office space. Shi stared off into space as if thinking when he would need to move to his own building.

I asked Shi about the research climate in China and overall innovative abilities of Chinese researchers. "Overall innovation is not yet as good in China as the United States," he conceded, "but it is definitely getting better. On both the academic and industry sides, China is catching up quickly in innovation and technology. For example, one of the hottest areas in biotech in the world is antibody drug conjugates, and the Chinese company ADC is making great strides."

As Shi spoke, he beamed with an electric positivity. He had the energy, optimism, and excitement of entrepreneurs who feel that anything is possible and that nothing can stop them. For a biotech researcher in China, his bright outlook surprised me. I had thought he would be more pessimistic.

China was not supposed to be a scientific innovator. Pundits such as Bloomberg's William Pesek argued Chinese government's heavy regulatory hand and the lack of a robust Internet stifle innovation in China. Vivek Wadhwa, vice president of academics and innovation at Singularity University, wrote an influencer piece for

LinkedIn in November 2013 arguing that the Chinese "government's efforts are hampering innovation rather than fostering it."[1]

The caliber of research happening in RuiYi's facilities seemed to belie Pesek's and Wadhwa's arguments. I wanted to know if Shi agreed with their premise about the government standing in the way.

"The government actually is not the problem holding back innovation in biotechnology," he said. In fact, he elaborated, the government was "actively promoting innovation in the sector, giving lots of financial backing and subsidies to companies in the form of grants, access to facilities, and equipment."

He leaned back for a moment and said, "Importantly, they are also letting private companies form potential collaborations with the academic community, which opens up all sorts of opportunities."

Biotech research received support from the most powerful quarters. For example, Shi pointed to the mission to make the newly established university Shanghai Tech, run by Jiang Mianheng, the son of former president Jiang Zemin (one of the so-called princelings), to become the Caltech of China. Resources are being poured into the school to create an environment conducive to research and development.

One reason RuiYi set up operations in Shanghai in addition to California was precisely because the climate was so good in China, while deteriorating in America. Shi elaborated, "The Obama administration's budget cuts are decreasing funding in scientific research," whereas the opposite was true in China. "The opportunities are great, with so many Chinese scientists coming back from overseas and strong support from the government." Flourishing contract research organizations (CROs), such as Wuxi PharmaTech and Viva, to which big pharmaceutical companies, such as Pfizer, Merck, AstraZeneca, Novartis, Genentech, and Millennium, outsource research, were also important, because they gave many researchers on-the-job training and increased the knowledge and skill level of the workforce.

In Shi's eyes, the main obstacle to true innovation in biotechnology lay not with burdensome government regulations, or even lack of talent, but financing. Similar to the early days of the information technology field—perhaps even more so—health care and biotech investors in China have a strong bias toward easy-to-grasp business models and opportunities for quick turnarounds. It's the low-hanging fruit problem all over again, and there still is plenty to pluck in China's health care sector, where great opportunities abound to make cheap but good enough medical devices from companies as well as generic drugs.

A key problem lies in the backgrounds of the investors themselves, Shi said. "Many of the investors in China are smart but they just don't understand biotechnology. Often they come from business or government backgrounds rather than from science backgrounds, where they truly understand the underlying research." The situation is very different from America or Europe, where investors typically have research backgrounds, he said. "They understand what we are doing and are able to give good advice during board meetings, but most investors in China don't really understand the real research."

Shi paused and then said, "But despite the challenges, innovation is definitely coming to China and the situation is improving. And the government is helping spur innovation, not hurting it."

∞

Unlike in America and Europe, a split is in the innovation taking place in biotechnology and the traditional health care field in China. Although biotech is seeing innovation as Shi outlines, the market demands in health care are more basic.

Expansion of basic health care coverage is viewed as a necessary ingredient in China's new growth model of making services and consumption account for a larger proportion of the economy. Without better health care coverage, everyday Chinese won't feel secure enough to spend more money.

One of the key barriers preventing many Chinese from spending more has been the lack of a social safety net, much of which was taken away during the reform and opening-up period of the 1980s, which got rid of the iron rice bowl where the state provided job security, housing, income, and medical benefits.

Many Chinese do not have adequate health insurance, and care is out of reach for most *laobaixing,* or ordinary people. People are forced to save in case of a rainy day, with many extended families pooling to care for a sick loved one. CMR's research found people older than age 50 often save 60 percent or more of their salaries because of fears of not being able to pay for medical costs.

To address the situation, the government is implementing and enforcing better health coverage laws for workers. By 2011, about 95 percent of Chinese—roughly 1.2 billion people—had access to basic health care compared with a mere 30 percent in 2003 as the government opened more basic hospitals and clinics at the municipal and village levels and was allowing for more private investment into hospitals. As a result, opportunities abound for the first time for non-state-owned entities, which is why capitalists, such as Rob McCormack at Mustang Ventures, are so keen on investing in them.

Innovation in the health care sector remains limited because there is simply so much low-hanging fruit because budgets are being spent on basic needs. As more basic hospitals open and as the government removes price caps on some procedures, spending is shifting toward essential purchases, such as x-ray and ultrasound machines.

Previously the government bought the newest and best medical devices from around the world—often top-of-the-line computerized tomography (CT) scan and positron emission tomography (PET) scan machines from big names, such as General Electric (GE), Siemens, and Philips—to show how advanced Chinese hospitals were. But that is changing because the focus is now more on spreading health care coverage than on flagship hospitals.

Coinciding with the corruption crackdown, there has been a change in procurement processes. Committees composed of local Ministry of Health (MOH) officials and hospital department heads are handling medical device purchases at the city or county level for multiple hospitals at once to negotiate better prices for large-volume orders for devices, such as patient monitors, hematology analyzers, and ultrasound machines.

Investments are being directed toward domestic companies, such as Mindray Medical International, Edan Instruments, Biolight and China Resources Wandong Medical Equipment, that improve the quality gap between domestic and foreign players, such as GE and Philips. These firms focused more on merely good enough quality, where the low-hanging fruit is right now, than true innovation. This focus is working. As Dr. Jaeson Lee, a doctor at St. Michael Hospital in Shanghai, told me, "Chinese medical device companies are as good but cheaper than Western companies for low-end equipment and are catching up at the high end."

Foreign players are being boxed out of the procurement process because of high prices and weak distribution, so the real opportunities are for Chinese companies or for foreign investment in Chinese firms.

❧

I know pain. When I was in high school, I had back surgery because of a sports injury and had to be in a body cast for a full year. My school bought La-Z-Boy recliners for each of my classrooms for me to recline during class because I could not sit up easily. After I got out of the body cast, I was generally okay for a few years. Then one day, when I was 25 and at the end of my honeymoon, I heard a pop in my ankle suddenly while walking in Repulse Bay in Hong Kong. I could no longer walk any distance longer than 10 feet without searing pain.

For the next five years, I had to use crutches or a cane to get around. I even took wheelchairs when traversing China's cavernous airport terminals because I could not handle the distance from the check-in counter to the gates. The pain and lack of mobility really affected how I thought about the world—I became more sympathetic to the plight of poor Chinese without medical coverage and started to think about e-commerce and online forms of entertainment that made it easier for me to live when I could not get around easily.

I went to 38 doctors. I became used to Chinese hospitals, and they are not pleasant places for everyday people. If you don't have lots of money to buy VIP time slots or connections to skip queues, you just have to grab a ticket and wait in line for hours to see a doctor. Patient rooms are often filled with dozens of other patients so privacy does not exist. The frazzled, overworked doctors in top-tier hospitals have so many patients to see that they often spend less than a minute per patient.

Unless a family member or friend had introduced us, or I paid out of pocket for VIP service, I didn't trust doctors in hospitals in China. If someone else didn't introduce us, doctors always seemed to want to do tests—even if another doctor had already done the same ones—or prescribe mounds of medicine. I once had a small rash on my wrist around my watchband, and I was prescribed $200 worth of medicine, for a problem that needed hydrocortisone cream only or would go away on its own in a few days.

Thankfully, I always had decent health care insurance to pay for those trips. But those weekly trips to the hospital gave me an up-close view of the massive corruption and poor treatment for everyday people in the health care sector.

Lily Lu, a poor 24-year-old woman from Anhui who earned $150 a month in 2013 told me, "Poor people in China cannot afford to get sick. We have no insurance and do not trust doctors." Lily spent a lot of time exercising and eating vegetables to boost her immune system and minimize trips to the doctor.

Another young woman, Jasmine, told me a doctor in a local Chinese hospital had once told her she had to spend the equivalent of half a year's salary to have a simple procedure done or else she would never be able to have a child. A friend of hers, who was a foreigner, talked her into going to a Western-run clinic for a second opinion. "The foreign doctor told me the problem was minor and that it would go away on its own. It did in less than a week. Thank goodness I didn't listen to the Chinese doctor and spend all that money."

Over the past few years there has been a slew of attacks on doctors by frustrated patients. The Chinese Hospital Association found that on average each hospital in China had 27.3 violent incidents in 2012, up from an average of 20.6 violent incidents in 2008. There were more than 20,000 such incidents in China alone in 2013.

On March 23, 2013, in Harbin, a city in China's northeast, for example, a patient stabbed four hospital workers, killing one, because he complained he did not get immediate treatment. Physically attacking a doctor is never warranted, but even while not condoning the attackers' actions, I can still understand and sympathize with many of their grievances. In interview after interview with lower-income Chinese consumers about health care, I have heard the same sense of helplessness and anger at the medical system. Many ordinary people resent doctors and feel they overprescribe medicines and recommend unnecessary surgeries to get kickbacks and boost their incomes.

Part of the problem is that doctor pay is low, with many doctors earning less than $800 a month, even in large cities. Doctors feel they have to rely on kickbacks and bribes just to get by. One brain surgeon in Tianjin told me in 2002 that he made so little that he had to take bribes to pay for basic living expenses.

One stent distributor I interviewed in 2011, Mr. He, told me candidly, "Of course, I have to pay off doctors and hospital procurement managers. If I didn't, they would never buy my products." To get around laws in their home countries, such as the Foreign Corrupt Practices Act (FCPA) in the United States and similar laws in European countries, many multinational pharmaceutical and medical device firms collaborated with local distributors, often relatives of hospital administrators, and follow a kind of don't ask, don't tell policy. The firms would tell distributors and resellers, as well as end buyers, that they could not give bribes and then look the other way.

In 2013, the government began investigating British pharmaceutical giant GlaxoSmithKline (GSK) for paying millions in bribes to doctors. Many analysts, such as James McGregor, the head of the communications firm APCO Worldwide in China, claimed in an interview with the BBC the targeting of GSK was mainly an act by the government to show foreign companies "who is the boss." McGregor pontificated that the government behavior was "very worrisome" for foreign companies. But that is not really the case if one digs beneath the surface and understands how the central government under President Xi views its responsibility to everyday Chinese.

The driving factor behind the focus on corruption in health care has been people's welfare—not protectionism or to demonstrate power. Corruption was causing poor treatment and caused prices to soar to levels unaffordable for everyday Chinese. The government investigations targeted not only GSK but also Chinese companies and health care professionals to make the system fairer. Chinese doctors are regularly arrested for bribery.

The crackdown under President Xi has started to work. One man in Beijing told me in 2013 he tried to bribe a doctor to ensure the doctor did not intentionally botch back surgery for his mother but was rebuffed. The doctor told him she wouldn't take bribes anymore because she was too worried about being sued or arrested. Initially the man was actually worried the doctor wouldn't treat his mother as well because the doctor didn't get a bribe from him, but as he saw that she really was not taking any bribes from anyone, he thought the crackdown was good and much needed because the system was not fair and too corrupt.

The crackdown on corruption and reform of the health care sector in general also means there is more low-hanging fruit still to grab in the sector. Corruption in the procurement process gave edges to some companies that would not have gained market share if they had not doled out bribes for doctors. The result is that shady companies that had no competitive advantages beyond their willingness to bribe are being weeded out, and companies that have the best quality and value offers will be able to grab market share and make the market more efficient.

The government is also shifting spending toward smaller municipal-level hospitals rather than the most famous flagship hospitals. The result is a shift of spending away from the most expensive, high-tech machines to more affordable devices with good enough quality, often made by up-and-coming domestic brands, such as the kind Dr. Lee at St. Michael buys. As a result Chinese companies, such as Biolight and Edan, that offer affordable patient monitoring and life support devices are doing very well. Many investors focus more on grabbing low-hanging fruit in the health care sector rather than on investing in true innovation in biotechnology.

The major barriers to innovation in biotechnology and health care are the continued low-hanging fruit, which is diverting resources away from innovation, and the lack of an ecosystem in China of researchers, entrepreneurs, and financiers that understand underlying research and are willing to invest. But as Shi showed, that ecosystem is growing as more Chinese return from overseas to conduct research and as CROs flourish and provide on-the-job training.

Brett Tucker, Managing Partner, Baird Private Equity China

Brett Tucker, a graduate of the Wharton School and the Lauder Institute of the University of Pennsylvania for his BA, MA, and MBA, has been doing business in China for the past 18 years. He has lived in Shanghai for 11 of those years. In 2003, he opened Baird's first office in China to assist Baird's U.S. and European portfolio companies operationally. In 2007, along with his partner Huaming Gu, he cofounded Baird's Chinese investment business, developing the strategy, raising the money, and hiring the team. He has made 11 investments in China and had his first two exits (one trade sale and one initial public offering).

Rein: Baird is investing heavily in the health care and consumer sectors. What opportunities do you see best for growth in the coming decade?

Tucker: Ultimately, the positive macro trend behind our investment thesis in both these sectors is essentially the same—the rising incomes and expectations of the Chinese middle class—and we always try to make sure our portfolio companies will somehow benefit from those factors. It is clear that Chinese consumers are demanding higher-quality, more innovative consumer products. However, what may not be as obvious is, as their incomes rise, they are also demanding, and can pay for, higher-quality health care beyond the state-owned system. In health care this is best exemplified by the high percentage of health care costs that are paid out of pocket. In China, around 40 percent of health care costs are paid by patients out of pocket, compared with far lower percentages in Western countries. Patients and their families understand the benefits of the higher-quality health care products and services and tens of millions of them have the money to pay for them, whether they are drugs, devices, or procedures. We even see this in our diagnostics company, where they pay for more sophisticated tests out of pocket.

However, whether it is a health care or consumer investment, we have found a recipe for success is to take a proven business model that has worked in other parts of the world. There is no need to reinvent the wheel in China to make an attractive investment return. Find a proven business model and then a local management team that knows how to tweak and adjust the model so it will work in China. Sure, truly innovating a new business model in China can drive even higher returns, such as what we are seeing in social media and the Internet sector in China. However, with this approach comes more risk, so depending on your investment needs, tweaking a proven model for China can drive attractive risk-adjusted returns.

Rein: Please give examples of your health care investments and the underlying reasons why you invested.

Tucker: The first of our three health care investments in China was in a CRO called Frontage, which we have exited. Our second is a reference lab called Kindstar, a leading player in China's higher-end esoteric diagnostics space. The company is growing and has a lot of open space in front of it.

The third investment is in Shanghai-based Kedu Healthcare, the leading independent provider of maintenance service and spare parts for medical equipment used in hospitals. It has a talented and experienced management team that mostly came out of GE Healthcare, and is a trusted partner to several of the largest equipment makers in the world. As the market leader, Kedu has major scale . . . and an attractive recurring revenue model. What Kedu wanted from Baird Capital was for us to tap our overseas network in the United States and Europe and introduce them to other equipment makers that need a partner like Kedu on the ground in China.

Kedu is a good example of the way we like to invest, which is to find a market leader that is already growing nicely, and use our money and international resources to try to help it grow faster. China's private equity market is too competitive, so if we don't have an angle, such as these international resources, we will likely take a pass.

Rein: What opportunities are there for medical tourism from China to markets like South Korea and Thailand?

Tucker: This is a good example of a health care investment opportunity that is directly tied to rising incomes and expectations. I know several investors that are looking at and investing in this medical/surgery tourism space. Many believe most of this should and will come back onshore over time. However, there will always be a part of the market that wants to combine the procedure with the trip abroad, which is a different service. The Chinese outbound travel opportunity is a clear 20-year trend.

Rein: The government has set a goal of getting better health care to everyone throughout China. What is holding back development, and what opportunities are emerging?

Tucker: In general, access to some base level of health care for the masses is a higher priority than improving the quality of health care for the large middle class that is demanding and can pay for better care. Both access for the less fortunate and improved quality for the more fortunate are needed. My sense is the Chinese government will continue to prioritize access for the masses, not unlike the Obama administration's priority, and will do a nice job here and make progress. The bottleneck in improving access here will not be money, government desire, or the equipment—the hardware—but rather the software, meaning the volume of trained doctors, nurses, and hospital management to effectively absorb government investment and convert that into quality access. I can't tell you how many meetings I have had in China where a doctor or hospital administrator is very proud to show us their latest piece of expensive, cutting-edge hospital equipment. Then when we go to the clinical room where the equipment is located, it is either still in the box unopened or unattended and gathering dust because nobody knows how to operate it.

However, perhaps a more interesting opportunity for private investors than increasing access is improving the quality of health care for the rising middle class. It is the wide gap between this poor experience that a lot of middle-class people have and the health care experience my family has had in China that creates amazing opportunities. I believe the private sector will shrink this gap while the government will focus on increasing access. Middle-class Chinese in major cities are tired of this poor experience. They know what the experience should be and they have the money to pay for it. The state-owned health care system won't solve this problem, so we are trying to find the innovative companies that will, because China's middle class wants and deserves better.

Rein: How would you describe what it's like on the ground, investing and operating in China every day?

Tucker: Investing in China is very challenging and sometimes from the outside we make it look much easier than it is. I often joke that the fees and compensation we receive should be like gymnastics scoring, where we get both an execution and a degree of difficulty score. So far none of my investors agree with me and just tell me to get back to work, but I will keep trying.

I also often feel like one of those people with eight long sticks and plates spinning on the top of them. Getting deals done here takes a lot of time, patience, and persistence—our average time from meeting a business owner to closing is about 14 months. So you have to have a lot of plates spinning at once just to make sure you deploy capital at a reasonable pace. Then when a deal starts to wobble you have to give it another push to keep it spinning if you like it and want it to close.

Affordable Products

Hospitals—and the MOH—are changing how budgets are spent to crack down on corruption and ensure better coverage for lower-income Chinese. Worried about social instability arising from unaffordable medical care coverage, the government is allowing for more private hospitals and easing price caps on services. They are also pushing to green-light district-level hospitals in smaller cities to take care of minor problems and ease congestion at the most famous hospitals.

Instead of erecting flagship hospitals equipped with state-of-the-art equipment in tier-one cities, such as Shanghai, hospitals are purchasing more affordable domestic brand medical devices and equipment. They are also likely to raise doctor visit fees but prescribe fewer medicines.

Key Action Item: Health care spending will increase but expect a budget shift toward affordable domestic Chinese firms that offer good enough products at cheap price points. Long dominant Chinese and foreign players might need to acquire cheaper brands or launch new more affordable brands to ensure market share without deteriorating the main brand as discounting does.

Rising Medical Tourism

South Korea, Singapore, and Thailand have emerged as key destinations for Chinese medical tourism. Because most Chinese do not have great insurance, much of their spending is out of pocket, so they are more willing to go abroad for treatment than Americans, who are tied down to specific groups of doctors in specific regions.

South Korea is popular for cosmetic surgery, Singapore for umbilical cord blood, and America for cancer and other more serious treatments. Somewhat superficially, consumers determine where they go often because they see specialties based on television shows. Korean dramas featuring male and female actors who approximate the Chinese ideal of beauty are a big reason why Chinese consumers want to get plastic surgery in South Korea. Similarly, many Chinese learned about America's medical system from George Clooney and *ER* and *Grey's Anatomy*, so they want to go to the United States for life-and-death treatments.

Key Action: Target increasingly wealthy Chinese consumers, who look to travel for medical treatment to countries whose medical expertise they feel is stronger than China's. There still is higher trust in foreign products and medicines because of fears of counterfeiting in the medical sector and subpar bedside service. Product placements in popular movies or television series can also drive sales more meaningfully in China than in America, where advertising sways customers less.

Supplements and Older Chinese

Because of concerns about the high costs of medical care, many Chinese try to boost immune systems and limit doctor visits through consuming supplements. They also are concerned about the side effects of Western medicines. Older Chinese often trust traditional Chinese medicine or Western supplements more than Western medicines.

This creates a huge opportunity for over-the-counter supplements for arthritis, amino acids, and general immune system health.

Key Action Item: Target China's aging population with supplements rooted in traditional Chinese medicine. Today's retirees have little disposable income because they largely missed out on the economic reforms of the past three decades. But because of tight family networks, where retirees often live with their children, today 30- and 40-year-olds buy supplements for their parents. As today's 40-year-olds age, they are also buying more supplements.

4

THE INNOVATION CURVE STAGE 3

INNOVATION FOR THE WORLD

A gigantic oblong glass and concrete structure rises out of the middle of a rice paddy field like an alien spaceship, with white sand and crashing blue surf in the distance. I walk toward the building. The sun beats down, and a light breeze sways the palm trees lining the road. I am in Haiteng Bay in Sanya, the main resort destination city of Hainan Island, often nicknamed the Hawaii of China. I cannot remember ever breathing air this clean in China before, and I take it in using long, deep breaths as I walk.

The building is a hospital, the Hainan branch of the famous People's Liberation Army (PLA) 301 Hospital in Beijing. As I walk inside I pick up the distinctive half-swallowed *err* sounds of the Beijing accent echoing through the empty halls and lobby.

The chatter seems out of place; just as the building itself does, thousands of miles away from the capital. I walk into a patient examination room because I have a slight cough to find Dr. Peng waiting for me. He is in his late 30s, with a round face and the beginnings of a middle-aged man's paunch. He starts speaking, also with the strong err-inflected Beijing accent.

Most of the doctors in the hospital are from Beijing, Dr. Peng tells me, forced to move to Hainan for two-year rotations. He hardly sees any patients. In this hospital, unlike every other Chinese public hospital I have been to, wait times to see doctors are less than five minutes.

Dr. Peng tells me, "I don't want to be here, frankly, but the hospital is forcing all of us to come here. They need a good hospital to build up the area."

Building a key project in the middle of nowhere to jump-start growth in a new part of a city is a common approach the government takes to development in China. Typically the government will build or relocate a hospital, university, or headquarters for a state-owned enterprise to the middle of an area earmarked for investment and growth.

Over a 5- to 10-year period, the government slowly moves in other things: supermarkets, kindergartens, and office buildings. Slowly a community starts to emerge. It became a fad for Western news crews, such as *60 Minutes*, to visit these areas, take a few shots of a lot of empty streets and vacant buildings, and speak breathlessly in voiceovers of these harbingers of the Chinese economy's imminent collapse. Some of these reports went viral and were widely shared and commented on in Western news blogs and on YouTube. Famed short seller Jim Chanos saw the same signs, pointing to empty-looking cities, such as Chenggong, a new suburb of the Yunnan provincial capital Kunming, as bellwethers of a disaster on the scale of "Dubai times a thousand."

The reality of many of these sites is that they are simply projects with 5- to 10-year implementation plans. Many of the so-called ghost cities—including Chenggong—are now bustling cities.

One of the major real estate developers of a city the *Wall Street Journal* portrayed as being a ghost town in early 2014 told me when I asked his response to the article, "Of course the city is empty right now. That is part of a five-year plan. Until a state-owned enterprise ends its lease in another location and relocates at the end of 2014, of course it will be empty. The plan is for the city to slowly fill up, 20 percent of capacity annually for the next five years. If the city is empty still in 2020, then there is a problem." Of the original famous ghost towns Western media pointed out, only Ordos in Inner Mongolia remains a true ghost town. The others have slowly added populations.

The Hainan branch of the PLA hospital is one of the first initiatives to build up Haiteng Bay in Sanya. Part of an initiative to capture domestic tourism, 35 five-star hotels, such as the Conrad and the Westin, are being built within a short drive from the hospital, as are high-end housing projects and private yacht clubs. I would not be surprised if the government pushed retired officials and military officers to the hospital to seek medical treatment. Because it covers insurance, it could direct them to seek treatment in Hainan to help spur the area's growth.

Building centerpiece projects to develop an area is a common blueprint for local governments in China. I thought back to when I first saw Pudong, the massive zone east of Shanghai's Huangpu River, in the 1990s; it was just swampland.

To develop the Pudong New Area, the government first built the Oriental Pearl TV Tower in 1994, and in the late 1990s the Jin Mao Group built the pagoda-like 88-story Jin Mao Tower, China's tallest building at the time. Even after Zhu Rongji, China's prime minister at the time, convinced Thailand's wealthiest man, Dhanin Chearavanont, to build the Super Brand Mall, the area remained empty for years. Analysts scoffed, calling the area a white elephant.

"No one would ever work or live there," one skeptical Italian investor told me in 2003. "There's just too much overcapacity." But as congestion and high rents in Puxi—the area west of the Huangpu River—became unbearable, and facilities, such as subways, in Pudong started to improve, soon companies such as Morgan Stanley, DuPont, and Google relocated their offices to Pudong.

The local district government of Jinqiao in Pudong put up expat-friendly housing complexes with broad tree-lined roads reminiscent of American suburbs; added international schools, such as the Hong Kong-owned Yew Chung International School, the U.K.-curriculum Dulwich College, and U.S.-style Concordia International School; and pushed for French retailer Carrefour to add locations. Shuguang Hospital, a state-owned traditional Chinese medicine hospital, was relocated from the tony Xintiandi shopping area in Puxi to the Zhangjiang industrial park in Pudong, near Dr. Shi Lei's office.

The local government erected Shanghai's largest airport there and green-lighted the construction of China's tallest office building. The world's fastest magnetically levitating train line, which reaches speeds of more than 300 kilometers an hour and takes riders from faraway Pudong Airport to Century Park in 7 minutes, was also built. A decade later, the government approved a Disneyland resort and a new free-trade zone in the district.

Today, Pudong looms far from a white elephant. It has 5.2 million residents and some of the highest-priced real estate in the world. Similar projects with multiyear development plans are being undertaken throughout the country. For instance in the Binhai part of Tianjin, the government is creating a new office and entertainment area with Juilliard, the famed performing arts conservatory, opening a campus there.

The treatment offered by Dr. Peng and his colleagues was quite good and on par with concern given me in top hospitals in America. Leaving the hospital, I decided to look around at the surrounding neighborhood. It was beautiful. The beaches were long and natural. Tall trees stood at the beach's edge, and the government had restricted construction too close to the beach so as not to destroy the view of the shoreline.

Later that day I decided to look at some of the new housing compounds being built nearby. Clean air, the ocean, a good hospital nearby. I sent my wife a voice message on WeChat, saying it might be a good place to retire some day.

⋘⋙

The "build it and they will come" model for economic development has been hugely successful for China, so much so that it has been a continued impediment to the development of innovation.

For Chinese government officials, encouraging the development of new cities and suburbs over 10 years is an easy blueprint to follow. They find a small number of large real estate developers they trust, often owned by a state-owned company (as was the case with the Jin Mao Group in Pudong), to launch projects. The state-owned banks provide low-interest-rate financing. Developers build a subway, railroad, and other transport links to the new area and force state-owned enterprises to relocate their main offices to that area. The huge project can be easily controlled by ensuring when phases will start and what types of initiatives will be undertaken. Importantly, such large-scale projects provide simple tax collection and lots of employment.

Switching to an innovation-based economy is much harder for officials to understand and control for consistent growth.

Overseeing hundreds of thousands of start-ups is more difficult from a tax collection and growth estimate standpoint than overseeing a few big state-owned enterprises. An economy that actively promotes innovation simply strains the bureaucracy more. More risk exists for an official to get in trouble if he or she green-lights a company that later is found not to be politically reliable.

Local governments have become addicted to easy oversight and tax collection by focusing on heavy-investment and big infrastructure projects, such as airports and railroads. If local gross domestic product (GDP) growth drops, they just force banks to increase credit to favored developers. It also explains why local governments are reaching dangerously high levels of debt and reliance on land sales for tax revenue.

If it can sometimes be hard for financiers to understand innovation and be willing to take risks, it is even harder to get local government officials, who are often more skilled at moving up the political ladder than at concrete economic skill sets, on board. For the past 30 years, a large component of government officials' performance measurement (and therefore chances for promotion) has been based on GDP growth. Officials simply do not want to take risks that could endanger their chance of being promoted, or, even worse, show their incompetence if they end up promoting the wrong type of innovation.

Expanding a tier-one city, such as Shanghai, or a scenic vacation spot, such as Haitang Bay, is more sustainable than the building going on in some lower-tier cities. The government risks running into overcapacity in some markets and needs to ensure that buyers and businesses move into some of the newer developments or else some of these developments will become ghost towns.

Aside from a bureaucracy that is not set up to promote innovation, I wanted to find out more about the future development of and challenges for innovation in China. I wanted someone who had experienced a big scope, someone who had served as an operator in a large business but who also invested across different industries.

I asked many leading businesspeople who I should interview—one name kept popping up, David Wei, the former chief executive officer (CEO) of Alibaba.com, the business-to-business (B2B) platform of Alibaba, who now runs the private equity firm Vision Knight Capital. One of Wei's limited partners in Vision Knight told me, "Wei's fund has some of the best returns in Asia in the past five years and is one of the savviest investors in China."

From afar, I had always been impressed with Wei's investing prowess and how he built up Alibaba. I arranged to meet with Wei one spring day in 2014 at Vision Knight's offices in the Kerry Center near Century Park in Pudong.

⚯

I got stuck in traffic getting to Wei's office and was 40 minutes late. I'd called his assistant repeatedly while stuck in traffic, and she kindly said not to worry. However, I fretted someone of his stature would be too busy to wait or would take my lateness as a slight. I have found many of China's most successful businesspeople and government officials feel slighted easily if seated at the wrong place at dinner or if they do something that they perceive as a loss of face, and Wei is one of China's most successful businesspeople and investors.

After leaving Alibaba in 2012, Wei's former boss and Alibaba founder, Jack Ma, was Wei's first investor in his $250 million fund. Richard Li, the son of Asia's richest man, Li Ka-shing, also was one of the earliest investors. In just two years, Vision Knight has invested in 10 firms and exited three, including a trade sale of 91 Wireless, a smartphone app distribution platform, to Baidu for $1.9 billion. When I talked to him, he had already raised a second fund of $550 million.

But as I entered Wei's office, I realized I was wrong to worry. He was as gracious and understanding as could be, almost princely as he stood erect and told me not to worry. He smiled, said, "Welcome," and motioned me to sit on a plush white couch. His office had a warm, almost homey feel with the waiting area looking like a living room. There was a set of couches around a tea table with a plate of candy, in stark contrast to the cold, antiseptically modern look of most private equity (PE) fund offices I'd been to in China, which had lots of glass and metal fixtures. Wei said he wanted anyone who visited him to feel comfortable and at home.

As soon as Wei started talking, I could see he had the spark that I had seen in entrepreneurs such as Gary Wang at Tudou. Wei was confident, hugely successful, yet humble. The graduate of Shanghai International Studies University and the London Business School recognized what he was good at but, more important perhaps, knew what he did not know.

He explained his firm focused on Internet, e-commerce, and Internet-driven B2B services, because those were the specific areas where his and his partners' expertise lay. He said that although he was bullish on other sectors as well—the health care sector was very attractive, for example—he admitted he would not invest in them for now because they were outside the areas of his current team's expertise.

Unlike many investors I have found in China who seemed to grab at any good idea, no matter how little they actually knew about it, Wei remained single-minded and focused. He seemed to have a well-thought-out, methodical reason for everything he did, from the décor of his office made to make people feel at home to why his fund is different from others to his investing strategy.

As I took a sip of coffee, Wei proceeded by telling me how he differentiated his firm from others—he combined the approaches of Bain Consulting and Bain Capital, using what he called a *freemium* model. Much like a consulting firm such as Bain, Wei and his colleagues, all experts in their fields, advised potential portfolio companies as clients on how to grow gratis—that was the *free* side. The *premium* side of the freemium equation was that, in return for his team's consulting advice, Vision Knight got to invest in the companies on exclusive basis or at lower valuations than other firms could get.

In other words, Wei positions himself as the smart money—he is not just throwing capital around but actually helping build companies up, and sweetening the deal for himself and his limited partners as he does so. Many other PE firms, I have observed in China, talk a good game but rarely carry out what they say. They put capital in but take a fairly hands-off approach often because the investors have little operating experience and are more deal makers with backgrounds rooted in investment banking. Wei and his colleagues set themselves apart from other PE firms—they get their hands dirty and help portfolio firms.

Wei started to explain to me his idea of "the spirit of the Internet," which he said was the backbone of his investing thesis. Wei began by telling me his approach to segmenting Chinese consumers, which was different from how most define the market. Rather than breaking consumers into separate groups by age or region as is standard, he said he threw out everyone born before 1985 and focused just on the *post-85s*. All his portfolio companies target this group, and no one else.

"In my experience, people who were born before 1980 are not the real Internet population in China," he said. I asked what he meant—after all, weren't hundreds of millions of Chinese born before 1985 accessing the Internet daily, too? He shook his head and said, "The real Internet population is people born after 1985. January 2000 was the real beginning of China's Internet. None of the key Internet players were really born before that. There were only about 4 to 5 million Internet users in China then, while there were 130 million in the United States. The people born between 1980 and 1985 had already completed their education in college by 2000. They mostly started using the Internet in a working environment."

Wei's analysis made sense to me so far. He continued, "People born after 1985 grew up with the Internet. They live with it. They use it for shopping, entertainment. Younger Chinese just do not go to supermarkets to shop—they either go to convenience stores or shop online. Everything else they just click." As for people who were born before 1985, it is hard to convince them to shift away from ingrained habits, such as shopping in brick-and-mortar stores.

He summed up his theory: "Targeting the post-85s' Internet behaviors are our investing strategy and how they approach the Internet is 'the spirit of the Internet.'" For instance, his portfolio firm 91 Wireless, an Android app marketplace, allows consumers to download and utilize the newest apps for gaming, social networking, and e-commerce, in other words the vital everyday components for young Chinese to entertain themselves and live. Another example is Wei's investment in Golden Ladies Photo, the country's largest wedding photo chain. The post-85s are just starting to marry and want to capture their weddings in photos to share with friends online. Consumers often spend months of their salaries on taking wedding photos, often traveling to exotic destinations just to take photos.

The wider implications for Wei's focused approach is critical: First, companies and investors need to understand consumers truly to segment the market properly because segmenting consumer groups purely based on five-year age brackets or region and socioeconomic status, as many analysts do, does not work in

China, and second, businesspeople need to understand that in China even a few years' difference in age means dramatically different consumer expectations and habits.

My fingers started to hurt; I was taking notes so fast because Wei's words were so insightful that I did not want to miss anything. I asked about the historical development of innovation in China. Wei argued that originally Chinese companies copycatted before progressing to innovating for China because it was a natural stage of development. When he was running Alibaba, there were still easy wins to have, and fears of property infringement forced most entrepreneurs to go for the quick buck. But from his vantage point as an investor, the market has developed to the stage where it is lucrative to invest in innovation. A great example of this type of investment would be 91 Wireless.

But he said, "The next step which will happen within the next five years is that Chinese firms will innovate for the rest of the world. It is starting to happen even now."

He told me a story of visiting London and meeting senior officials who advise the prime minister. "They asked me for my WeChat ID," he said. He said that they told him that a Chinese friend had gotten them hooked on WeChat and that they were now regular users. I have heard similar stories when visiting Indonesia and even South Africa—Chinese introduced WeChat to foreign friends, who then started using the service among themselves.

Another example of Chinese companies becoming global players would be Wei's investment in JNBY, a leading designer apparel brand. Originally focused on China, Wei tells me, the brand is now selling in Galeries Lafayette in Paris and Selfridges & Co. in London. It has also opened stores in New York and Tokyo, and the brand is pushing to create new designs to become a global player.

What were the challenges to continued innovation, I asked? One of the big challenges, Wei said, is executives did not feel safe because of lack of intellectual property and property rights so they went after quick returns. For instance, shop owners often left stores ramshackle because they worried the government would demolish stores in urbanization campaigns with little monetary compensation. Why spend money decorating a store if it would be knocked down in a few years? The situation was even more apparent when tens of millions were necessary to invest in research and development.

However, Wei said, the market is maturing, and innovation was increasingly being rewarded financially, making the risks were worth it. He pointed to the huge success of the sale of 91 Wireless to Baidu. "We could have gone public, but the trade sale valuation was too good."

The intensifying competition between Internet giants, such as his former company Alibaba, Baidu, and Tencent, was leading his firm to look for more and more innovative companies to acquire, he said, that were "good for entrepreneurs and for investors." The regulatory environment was improving but not as fast as the potential rewards from investing in innovation.

I asked what areas were most likely to have the greatest opportunities for Chinese firms to hit stage 3 on the innovation curve, where they innovate for the whole world. Wei believed opportunities would come from the mobile Internet space, where costs were lower and innovation could happen faster. Only a handful of programmers were needed to build something innovative in the mobile space.

He said mobile Chinese firms that catered to the post-85s were making pathbreaking changes in the mobile space. Examples of this burgeoning innovation include WeChat, as well as some shopping websites.

"Why do Chinese firms have an advantage over American firms in the space?" was my final question to Wei. He said that although most American Internet users got their first experience of the Internet from their personal computers (PCs), in China many users' first experience with the Internet was via a mobile device. This is similar to how many Chinese leapfrogged landline phone technology and went straight to cell phones in the late 1990s.

The top Internet players in China are developing with the mobile experience in mind from the very beginning. This contrasts with many American players, such as Facebook and Twitter, which are tweaking their PC interfaces for the mobile devices, a fine distinction but critical. WeChat is a good example of this innovation and risk taking. Tencent dominated with its PC-to-PC messaging system called QQ, but instead of tweaking QQ to work for the mobile phone, it started WeChat as a brand-new product.

Wei was right—there have not been dominant, innovative Chinese Internet players. Most have copycatted their way to success. Now that innovation is being rewarded financially, the newest entries are focused on the mobile device. In America, where technology innovation was born, dominant companies in PCs, such as Microsoft, are trying to enter the mobile world to grab opportunities but also need to balance new opportunities with maintaining revenue from a PC world.

There are very real continuing challenges to innovation in China, as outlined so far. During my interviews for this book, two other key areas emerged as barriers.

First, many respondents mentioned a weak education system that focuses too much on rote memorization and not enough on creativity as a barrier to innovation. Most saw that the education system was reforming with a greater emphasis on debate in the classroom but that it was taking too long to help industry in the short term. Executives wanted universities to use curriculum that was more applicable to real-world situations. However, many respondents said so many Chinese were studying abroad now, or that leading institutions, such as Duke University and New York University, were building campuses in China, that the top talent was getting access to the best innovative education opportunities before returning to China to put theory into practice. Enrichment schools, such as weekend art schools for children, were also proliferating and encouraging creativity that was lacking in the official school system.

Second, the lack of enforcement of intellectual property rights was also reported as a major problem. Many respondents said that it was not worthwhile to invest in innovation because other companies would steal their intellectual property without enough recourse. Respondents said court judgments would often get the right result, but damages were so small that they did little to dissuade unsavory businesspeople from infringing and paying small fines. Courts also did not have enough enforcement powers. The innovation that did take place was often in sectors such as mobile, where heavy investment and long-term investing horizons were unnecessary.

In spite of the barriers, many of the world's most innovative companies, such as Tencent and Alibaba, are in China. For the most part, they are in stage 2 of the innovation curve, where they innovate specifically for the Chinese market. But over the next five to 10 years, China will move to stage 3 of the innovation curve and start to focus on innovating for the world. Ambitious entrepreneurs see the opportunities to become global players and financiers see the potential returns.

Thomas Tsao, the Harvard-educated founder of Gobi Ventures, an early-stage venture capital firm that manages five funds, told me that as Chinese entrepreneurs "start challenging Silicon Valley–based start-ups to serve the international audience, globalization of Chinese innovations and technologies will be one of the most exciting investment opportunities in the next 20 years."

But who is most likely to engage in innovation and propel the country to stage 3 of the innovation curve is different in China. Unlike in America, where innovation develops from disruptive start-ups in Silicon Valley, most innovation in China will come from larger private Chinese companies. These companies have the consistent income coming in from divisions, such as online games, that rely on low-hanging fruit so they can take more risks. They also have the ability and cash to build trust with and lobby regulators.

China has moved from stage 1, the copycat stage, to stage 2, where innovation for the China market, often in the form of business model innovation, is taking place. The world had better get ready for the next stage, stage 3, where Chinese companies innovate for the world, because it coming fast.

S. Y. LAU, PRESIDENT OF ONLINE MEDIA GROUP, SENIOR EXECUTIVE VICE PRESIDENT, TENCENT

I first met the Harvard Business School–educated Lau in 2006 soon after he joined Tencent, when we both sat on the advisory board for ad:tech China, an interactive advertising and technology conference and exhibition. In his 20-year career in China, he previously had been the managing partner of Publicis China and the CEO for BBDO China.

Since meeting Lau, I have marveled at the growth he helped usher at Tencent. Known initially as an online and instant messaging company, Lau has helped build Tencent into one of the most innovative Internet firms in the world, with subsidiaries providing mass media, entertainment, Internet, and mobile phone value-added services.

In 2011 *Advertising Age* named Lau one of the world's 21 most influential people in marketing and media. I interviewed Lau to find out how Tencent had created a culture of innovation and what the keys to his success were.

Rein: How has Tencent fostered a culture of innovation?

Lau: A key thing is the diversity of Tencent's top management team. Diversity is certainly an ingredient for innovation, but it would remain just an idea if the founders of the company did not have an open-minded attitude, as well as hearts big enough to embrace differences. That emotional maturity is a rare leadership quality that I see in Pony Ma (the founder of Tencent), one that is not easily found in other local Chinese companies.

In addition to the open-mindedness in embracing diversity, three other key drivers that come into my mind, would be (1) a strong corporate belief in delivering the best user experience as our very core reason of being and mandate, (2) a consistent strong sense of insecurity within the top leadership team, and (3) the existence of a strong work ethic and a self-driven willingness to continuously learn and unlearn new things among the top performers in the company.

Rein: How do you implement these three key drivers within the company?

Lau: All Tencent employees know that a commitment to innovation is not a short-term KPI (key performance indicator) or project-driven mission. It has to be so deeply ingrained in the culture and soul of the company via a systematic and consistent inculcation program. If you were to ask anyone of our 30,000 people what our single most important mission is, I'd bet my last dollar that each one of them would say it's the user experience. In our day-to-day discussions with our people, the phrase *user experience* is used all the time. People are promoted and reprimanded largely based on their contribution toward making our user experience better.

We are no longer operating in a simple winner-takes-all scenario. The social interaction element of the Internet business underscored the possibility of any gifted talent that could take down a corporation that moves too slowly. We need to be really on our toes so that our commitment to providing best-in-class user experience is understood and practiced by all, not just a slogan. Such strong sense of urgency is a key trait within the Tencent leadership team.

Collectively, we recognized and consciously believe that the only way to stay relevant to your users and potential new users is through innovation. We did make some mistakes along the way. For example, close to a decade ago, we thought the magic formula for fostering the culture of innovation was to set up an innovation center. As time went by, we realized that the responsibility of innovation was too important to be left to a few engineers in an isolated group to manage. It was far more important to inculcate the responsibility and motivation for innovating within each product manager and engineer at the front line, as they are the ones that are in closer contact with our users.

Rein: What are the challenges to innovation and growth in China?

Lau: Human capital is a big challenge. By historical and learning habits, Chinese are more prone to following orders. Although we have witnessed drastic changes in such a generalized phenomenon in the recent years, the focus of the general workforce is still pretty much execution-centric.

The next challenge is the severe lack of respect for intellectual property (IP) protection, and a lack of contemporary legal system that ensure violations of the law are given commensurate punishment. In the recent NPC (National People's Congress) session, the chairman of Baidu was quoted saying that the current legal system was not well equipped to protect companies against IP crime in an adequate manner. He articulated the painful experience whereby a company with a market cap of more than 100 billion RMB (renminbi), when being prosecuted for such crime, would be likely to be fined only a couple hundred thousand RMB.

Rein: Do you see the greatest competition coming from domestic Chinese brands or foreign players?

Lau: Competition comes from everywhere in China. The Internet industry is such that whoever is able to provide a better product with better user experience is rewarded with followers or users. Plus, Chinese netizens are not as brand loyal as you might think. Take the video business for example. People would go to any video provider as long as the dramas that they were interested in were aired there. The users will always have a choice. The rapid speed of product development in recent years has helped nurture a new breed of consumers that demand for more, but are not necessarily willing to pay more. Because there will always be some new provider that is willing to absorb the cost and sacrifice profitability in the name of a potential IPO (initial public offering).

Align Your Interests with Chinese Companies

The government takes counterfeiting in the medical sector more seriously than in other sectors, such as software. For instance, the former head of the China Food and Drug Administration, Zheng Xiaoyu, was executed for corruption in 2007 because his infractions directly hurt people, whereas many street corners are lined with vendors selling pirated DVDs, unmolested by police.

As the domestic information technology industry comes into its own and is hit by piracy and IP infringement, the government is improving protection of IP rights. DVD vendors are being arrested in raids or having product confiscated. Circumstances are similar to those in Japan and South Korea in the 1960s to 1980s, where the governments did not enforce IP rights actively until domestic Japanese and South Korean firms were the ones losing money.

Key Action Item: Instead of accusing China of lacking morality, as Ted Laguatan did in a 2013 column for the *Inquirer* in the Philippines, Western brands should align with Chinese firms that have something to lose. Alibaba's Taobao marketplace has cracked down on IP infringement because it has much to lose if consumers lose faith in the genuineness, so selling on that platform makes sense.[1]

There is more money for the domestic firms to adhere to international standards than ever before, and the government moves quickly to protect their rights.

5

THE BEIJING COUGH

JANUARY 2013

Where do we eat?" I asked my colleague Ben Cavender. I looked across the street into a wave of blackness. We were standing in Beijing's central business district. The China World Hotel owned by the Shangri-La Hotel chain should be right across the street, I thought to myself, but I could see only a wall of smog.

Cavender threw me a look as if to say, "I can't believe this situation." Educated at the famed Phillips Exeter Academy and then Cornell University, where he rowed, he was my first hire at the China Market Research Group (CMR) in early 2006. He and I have been through a lot of struggles and challenges together as we have built up CMR. He is not easily perturbed. More like a rock. But at that moment, even he looked dismayed.

Cavender and I had just finished delivering a five-year growth strategy project for a business-to-business food service catering company. Both the headquarters of the firm in America and the president of the Chinese operation received the project well.

We wanted to celebrate with a nice meal. That happiness was soon replaced by shock as we went outside to look for a place to eat.

We could not even see 20 meters ahead, the air was so black and gritty. Ben and I were engulfed in what eventually became called Airpocalypse Beijing 2013, when the air quality topped 700 on the Air Quality Index (AQI), more than 30 times worse than World Health Organization (WHO) recommended levels.

To put this into context, the grit was double the 300 levels that hit Singapore during its national state of emergency in 2013 from Indonesian forest fires. Los Angeles, America's most polluted big city, usually tops off at around a 20 AQI reading. Paris declared a state of emergency in March 2014 when the AQI hit 150 and banned half of the city's cars from the road.

The Daily Show host Jon Stewart poked fun at Beijing's pollution, saying one could actually chew the air. Stewart was not far off. But for people living here and increasingly throughout the Asia-Pacific region, it is no laughing manner.

Air pollution is so bad that it is changing how people live, think about life, and prioritize spending. One of the top three reasons CMR has found e-commerce is soaring in China, for instance, is people do not want to go outside to shop as much. They limit walking on streets to shop because they fear grit entering their lungs. Generations have never actively exercised outdoors.

They cocoon themselves inside, preferring delivery people to hazard the air. Delivery people's pay is increasing to reflect the dangers. One wife of a delivery person from Jiangsu told me her husband makes $1,200 to $1,500 a month, up from $150 five years ago, because "It is such a hard job these days with pollution."

More than food and product safety, pollution is emerging as the main concern in life for Chinese, based on CMR surveys throughout the country. Online grocery shopping, for example, has largely failed in America despite the initial hype around concepts such as Amazon Fresh and online grocer Peapod, but in China it is taking off. As one 38-year-old Shanghai woman with two kids told me, "I just order from Sam's Club online. Why would I go outside in that?" she asked while pointing at the air outside through sludge-streaked windows.

Every year my firm surveys 5,000 people in 15 cities. In 2013, for the first time since CMR started the surveys in 2007, concerns over pollution became one of the top-five fears for consumers. Anxiety over pollution is changing not only what products people buy and how they buy them but also their willingness to live in China. Marc van der Chijs, the cofounder of Tudou, still does business related to China but relocated to Vancouver in 2011 because of concerns over pollution and food safety.

"The main reason," van der Chijs left, he told me, is "because of air pollution, I just felt I could not do this to my kids anymore. They often could not play outside, not even at school."

Understanding China's pollution problems and their effect on the economy and consumer habits might be the most critical area for businesspeople and investors to analyze. More than anger over corruption, pollution could cause social instability if parents are fed up at the impact on their children's lives. Curbing pollution (or the direct results of it, such as brain and capital drain) could cause the economy to slow, causing a rippling effect globally.

On the positive side, the pollution problems facing China remain so serious that the country stands as the leader in renewable energy innovation. David Victor, director of the University of California at San Diego's Laboratory on International Law and Regulation told the *Wall Street Journal* in 2011 that the combination of funding and willingness to embrace new solutions and technologies allows for more commercial development of innovations in China than anywhere else.

∝⃝

By no means is pollution a new problem facing China. By 2003 the air and water quality had deteriorated for a long time, and I criticized the situation then in writings and speeches. At the time I was still at Inter-Asia, and I'd been looking to invest in an air purifier company and a heart disease project and had found terrible mortality numbers stemming from pollution.

I spoke with a prominent Chinese government official about the situation. He scoffed at me, "The pollution problems in China are the same as the ones that Japan and Korea faced when their economies were developing. What about the smog in London in the early twentieth century?" He predicted the situation would be much better within a decade or so. "Only you foreigners from rich countries can afford to lecture us about pollution. Pollution is a natural offshoot of development and many Chinese are poor and are just struggling to put food on the table. You had to go through the same stage of pollution."

This is a common argument you hear in official defenses of the government's refusal to join global anticlimate change measures, such as the Kyoto Protocol. The nation is undergoing the same messy process all advanced countries went through as they industrialized, the argument goes, and it is unfair for developed countries to hold developing countries to a different standard. Those arguments do not really hold water anymore. The pollution numbers have gotten worse, not better, over the past 10 years, and the world has never seen so many people affected at one time.

University of California, Berkeley, postdoctoral researcher Stephanie Ewing reported the results of a six-month project in the

Environmental Science and Technology journal that 29 percent of particulate matter (PM) 2.5 lead in the San Francisco Bay area came from East Asia, mostly from China. Frustration is not just boiling over from foreigners or even wealthy Chinese, but Chinese at all socioeconomic levels.

Private car ownership in the last decade—China went from 6.5 million drivers on the roads in 2003 to 85 million in 2013, a 1,200 percent increase. This plays a major role in pollution, but much of the problem stems from the country's reliance for 70 percent of its energy needs on coal, one of the few natural resources China has in abundance. The result is that China spewed out more than 10 gigatons of carbon dioxide in 2014—more than America and Europe combined.

China's leadership is trying to address the problem, but doing so without causing the economy to slow too much remains difficult. Unfortunately the problem will likely deteriorate before it gets better.

Emissions in the United States, Japan, and other developed countries peaked when gross domestic product (GDP) per capita hit somewhere between $10,000 and $15,000. China's per capita GDP hovers around $6,000 now, suggesting emissions will continue to get worse at least until 2025 if incomes rise on average 7 percent a year, unless there is a major shift away from the country's reliance on coal.

I am always asked why pollution has emerged as such a big issue by consumers all of a sudden if pollution had been so bad for so long. The answer is a combination of two developments: First, the increased measuring and tracking of air quality data (specifically the AQI, for so-called PM 2.5 particles, the fine particulate matter small enough to get through the natural filters in humans' noses and get stuck in our lungs) has turned pollution from an abstract issue to a concrete one.

Second, the proliferation of smartphones has accelerated the spread of air quality data. At the end of the fourth quarter of 2012, Chinese phone makers, such as Huawei, Lenovo, and Xiaomi, started selling affordable smartphones using Google's Android platform. Companies started offering free apps tracking the AQI and allowing for easy sharing with friends on social media platforms, such as WeChat, and Sina Weibo. More than ever before people track pollution on an hourly basis, sharing with others in real time.

As the country urbanizes, people adopt lifestyles, such as eating more meat proteins and using more air-conditioning and other modern conveniences, that per capita create more pollution, not less. Part of the emerging Chinese dream includes a car and a large home with modern-day conveniences.

Pointing to other nations' pollution problems as they developed is no longer acceptable. It made sense in the 1990s, and even to some extent in 2003 when that official spoke to me, because even then many struggled to eat. But now the negatives of the growth-at-all-costs model are outweighing the benefits. More than 40 percent of deaths now relate to heart and brain disease because of pollution and fatty diets. China is now the second most obese nation after America.

Over the past few years, scores of wealthy Chinese have immigrated to other nations. Bain Consulting and other firms argue immigration numbers reached such high levels because wealthy Chinese worry about the economy. CMR's research contrasts with Bain's results. In interviews with several dozen Chinese worth $10 million or more in investable assets, we found Chinese primarily immigrate to get their families better access to education and health care and reduce exposure to pollution. In other words, the country faces a serious brain and capital drain as the nation's best and brightest flee to cleaner environments.

"What's your index say?" I asked my wife, Jessica. "Mine says 147." Jessica rolled over and checked her iPhone on the bedside table: 186 was her reading. She uses a smartphone app that collects and tracks air pollution readings from sensor equipment at the American embassy and consulates. The Chinese government apps tend to have better air quality readings, so we figure it is safer to go with the worse number just in case.

"What do we do today?" I asked, and we started to plan how to avoid the soupy air enveloping our home. Sometimes I feel like I am living on Mars in the Arnold Schwarzenegger movie *Total Recall,* where everyone stays indoors and taking a step outside could kill you. I joke, but it is a shameful state of affairs.

Whenever the AQI hits above 200, our answer is clear—instead of walking to school, I wrap my son up head to feet so that pollution does not get into his hair or on his skin. I secure a mask on his face, making sure it fits snugly, and drive him to school, which is a less-than-5-minute bike ride away.

When the AQI is at 120 (six times higher than recommended WHO levels) and below, we ride our bikes with masks on. We figure the benefits from the exercise offset the pollution's ill effects.

When the air quality falls between 120 and 200 is when the planning and guessing starts. The air remains hazardous but still breathable using an N95 filtering mask. We check the wind outside and scan the sky to see how thick the haze really is. If we think it may clear up in the afternoon and my son can play outside in his school's playground, we will bike over. If we think it will get worse, we take the car.

The whole time my heart hurts, wondering how I could expose my son to such an environment. Growing up in New Hampshire, I had snow days off from school; my son, Tom, has smog days.

Typically, at around 11 AM, my wife checks the AQI again. If it is okay, she and Tom will play outside after school. If it's bad, she will take him ice-skating or to some other indoor activity. If it is really bad, I have to drive home from work, pick him up, and take him straight home. We do not even want him in the car or a taxi driving outside to an indoor activity center because we worry pollution will seep into the car during the drive over.

The impact of pollution on people's lives goes well beyond extra respiratory ailments and skin conditions. It literally affects the planning of people's days and what consumers prioritize in life. One 28-year-old from Changsha in Hunan province summed it up well when she told me, "Who cares if I can buy Louis Vuitton bags if the water and air poisons me?" She has changed her spending from status symbols to products that protect her from pollution, such as masks and purifiers, and that boost her immune system.

Understanding how pollution affects day-to-day activities as well as life aspirations is critical for brands to adjust to the changes. It is also important for human resource departments to create policies dealing with pollution because of the effect on recruitment and employee retention.

Mr. Ma should be a happy man. He has what he calls his dream job, running the Chinese operations for one of the world's largest companies in the technology sector. Born in Taiwan, Ma received a master of business administration degree at the University of Chicago and joined his current company in California right after graduation. He quickly moved up the corporate ladder, and when the spot to run the Chinese operations opened up in 2009, his boss offered him the role.

Five years later, Ma and his family sat with mine in a Thai restaurant having dinner. "My company has made winning in China its main priority in the next decade," Ma told me as his four-year-old son ran over and grabbed his legs, laughing. He was cradling his 10-month-old son in his arms as he sucked on a Mickey Mouse pacifier.

The server brought over a plate of crispy, golden spring rolls with a tangy orange sauce on the side. To hit its goal of 30 percent revenue generated in China globally, Ma said, "I have been given great support from headquarters to invest in initiatives." He negotiated a high salary, with the company paying for housing, a car and driver, and international school tuition for his kids.

Yet despite his work satisfaction, Ma is considering leaving his position or asking for a transfer to a less high-profile position in a market such as Australia or New Zealand because he worries about pollution's effects on his children's health. So many Chinese have moved to Australia in recent years, which helps explains why *The Economist* says the country has the highest prices of any English-speaking nation.

Ma said, "Is it worth making all this money and working so hard if the pollution hurts my children? I'm not so sure anymore." His wife, Judith, nodded as Ma discussed the cons of staying in China.

She added the common refrain, "Maybe another year or two, then out of the country." They had thought about asking for a transfer to Hong Kong, but the pollution levels there were getting worse, too.

Ma and his wife are not alone in concerns about pollution. Debating whether to leave or stay, or how to reduce the risks of pollution, have become common topics for expatriates to discuss and are having a direct impact on organizations in recruiting and retaining talent. As for Ma's company, it might lose one of its top performers in a mission-critical market.

Japanese electronics giant Panasonic has started offering smog pay. The number of Japanese living in Shanghai, for instance, dropped from 57,458 in October 2012 to 47,700, a 17 percent drop, mostly because of pollution issues. The number of Japanese member businesses in the Shanghai Japanese Commerce & Industry Club actually rose 3 percent, indicating pollution and not Japanese-Chinese political tension caused the population decline.

Recruiting talent into China in the first place has emerged as a problem. Mr. Kim, a client who runs global marketing for a Korean powerhouse, messaged me, "I need your personal advice." He had just been offered an Asia-Pacific regional role based in Shanghai, running marketing for a hot Internet company with a package including a high salary, stock options, the works.

Kim told me did not know what to do. He wanted the job but wanted his son to be able to play soccer outside rather than in gymnasiums or under the domes some international schools install over playgrounds. He had already told the company he would be willing to be based in Hong Kong and fly into Shanghai weekly.

Understanding his concerns, the regional president he would report to was seeing if they could switch the offer to Hong Kong, underscoring the realities companies face when recruiting—they need to make accommodation because of pollution concerns. High-pay packages no longer suffice.

For the past decade a Chinese posting has been one of the hottest for ambitious, high-flying executives. But that is starting to change. Don Riegger, the global employer services leader in Asia for Deloitte and Touche, told me, "Quality-of-life considerations of living in China make it increasingly difficult to convince executives, particularly those with family, to accept a long-term assignment in China. The most critical locations are Shanghai and Beijing where pollution and concerns about the school system make China much less attractive. Companies still need to fill the need for specific executive talent in China but how they do that is getting more creative to adjust to lifestyle and family considerations."

Aside from affecting the human resource side of companies, firms catering to the expatriate community—English-speaking real estate agencies, international schools, and Western bars and restaurants—face tough times as more expats leave and others refuse to come. Where a few years earlier it was common for international schools to have six-month waiting lists for primary school admittance, many are now losing students or are being forced to spend millions installing air purifiers in every classroom. Costs to battle pollution are high but are now musthaves. One administrator at an international school in Shanghai told me she saw more departures than normal in January 2014. "The primary reason parents gave was pollution—not cutbacks in their companies." The number of students enrolled in Shanghai's two Japanese schools dropped to 2,912 from 3,175 a year earlier in April 2013.

Restaurants catering primarily to expatriates are also seeing lower foot traffic and must adjust menus to cater more to locals. The manager of one popular Western chain told me about his sales in 2014: "Expatriate foot traffic and spending has dropped but Chinese diners have increased." Local diners are looking for authentic experiences, but there are differences in preferred flavors and ordering styles (for example, more dishes that can be shared by groups rather than eaten individually), as we will see in Chapter 9.

Individual property owners renting to expatriate families are feeling the pinch, too. Many executives now come to China solo for a two- to three-year posting, leaving families in home countries. They need smaller spaces, often staying in serviced apartments rather than villas near international schools.

Joe, a Disney executive who is working on the planned Disneyland park in Shanghai, told me he chose to live in a serviced apartment rather than a villa because his family decided to stay in the States. "I'll be here for months at a time, rather than years."

Joe's situation is becoming more and more common. As Deloitte and Touche's Riegger expanded:

> Fewer multinational companies use the classic assignments where family moves together with the key executive to a foreign location for three to five years. The classic assignment has been replaced by short-term programs where the family stays home and the executive carries out their duties by extensive travel. They either stay in the location for up to 18 months with a liberal number of returns home or use an extensive series of business trips with a few weeks in China followed by a week or two back home. The short-term solution avoids the expense of moving the family but also the issue of the family adapting to what is perceived as an undesirable location due to significant pollution or weak and expensive education systems.

The next few chapters will examine how pollution affects spending and influences the conception of a new Chinese dream. Consumers are allocating budgets to experiences that make them happy, in part to overcome stress and depression stemming from pollution. They are also spending more on outlets that allow them to display self-expression and creativity as they reprioritize what is important to them. Pollution is now affecting nearly all facets of life.

PEGGY LIU, CHAIR OF JUCCCE

Peggy Liu is the chair of Joint United States–China Cooperation on Clean Energy (JUCCCE), a nonprofit that seeks to catalyze transformative change in the green movement of China by convening coalitions of cross-border and cross-sector influencers around precise collaborative action that triggers tipping points in sustainable energy, urbanization, and consumption. A graduate of Massachusetts Institute of Technology (MIT), Liu is an executive advisor to Marks & Spencer, as well as an advisor to the World Economic Forum Project Board on Sustainable Consumption and Volans and serves as a member of the Financial Times Stock Exchange Environmental Markets Committee.

As one of the leading voices on green living in China, Liu was honored as a World Economic Forum Young Global Leader, with the Hillary Step for climate change solutions in 2012, as a *Time* Hero of the Environment in 2008, as the Hillary Laureate of 2010 for climate change leadership, as one of *Forbes'* "Women to Watch in Asia" in 2010, as a *Huffington Post* "Greatest Person of the Day" in 2011, and as one of China's top 50 innovative business leaders by *China Business News Weekly* in 2012.

Rein: What needs to be done by the government to solve pollution problems?

Liu: Clearly the government recognizes the problem and is trying to rectify it. The issue is that pollution is multifaceted. You cannot just throw money at it and have it go away magically. Other countries took 20 to 30 years to fix their problems. In Los Angeles, where I was raised in the 1970s, people could not even see the mountains, even at times in the 1990s. Developed countries have historically taken 20 to 30 years to clean up the problem, and even then they did not get blue skies, but they did become more livable.

For China to tackle its pollution problem will probably take another 30 years. The problem, though, is where the situation is with climate change—we are getting to be quite late in the battle. China cannot take a normal course in history to tackle the issue. We need to accelerate in order to make sure we don't run up against very bad tipping points in climate change.

Rein: What is China doing to solve the problem?

Liu: When you look at different sources of pollution, coal power plants are one of the largest. Coal currently accounts for about 80 percent of electricity generation. The government hopes to bring it down to 66 percent over the next few years, which is quite a decrease. But the total amount of coal that will be used by that time will actually be triple current levels, so it is a relative decline, but not an absolute one.

China has to stop building new coal power plants. In 2013 the government committed $277 billion for three regions to combat air pollution and $330 billion for water pollution. President Barack Obama announced only one bill for a climate resiliency fund across all U.S. government agencies of only $8 billion. Compare the numbers to show how committed they are to the problem. Coal plants need to get more efficient. Coal is more stable than solar during the day or wind at night. The existing electric grid is being restructured to allow more variable energy inputs into the grid.

China has 28 nuclear power plants currently under construction, more than rest of world combined. They cannot be built too fast because we cannot have another Fukushima: We need to build them right. China already has the world's largest hydropower plant, Three Gorges Dam.

Cars are the second-biggest problem. That is why Beijing has had to reduce the number of license plates issued. Government officials cannot use official government car plates for personal reasons. Burning of agricultural waste and not turning it more efficiently into biomass. Small-homes that use wood fire to cook is also one of the issues. Coal use for heating is also a big issue.

The problem is a lot of stakeholders, different policies to address these issues fundamentally. Diesel trucks and low fuel standards for non-passenger-level vehicles like trucks or minitrucks are other issues.

Rein: What can ordinary people do?

Liu: The most important thing for consumers to do is to learn how to protect themselves. There is a myth that pollution is like a cold or eating germs, that the more you are exposed to it the stronger you get, but pollution is not like that. The more PM 2.5 particles get into your body the higher your chances of getting cancer. Eight-year-old girls are getting cancer.

The government used to give away coal for free in the north for home heating and now it is still heavily subsidized. There are 5.5 percent more deaths in northern China than the south simply because of the coal used to heat homes. Educating people on how they can think about pollution and protect family members is important. I kind of equate living in China to living on Mars. You really need to think about your environment—everything you are eating and breathing in every day, and how to make sure that the environment is within livable levels.

First, people need to wear (particulate-filtering) N95 masks a lot more regularly than they are doing now. WHO recommends a PMI 2.5 air quality index of 25 at maximum. Belgium stops all traffic when it hits 50. So why do people not wear their masks here? It is insane what we are doing to children and ourselves. People are affected by what they see others doing—if they see other people are not wearing masks, they won't either. JUCCCE started to give away N95 masks and push waterless urinals. Everyone should use wearable, washable masks that are sealed around the face and do not leak. Normal masks that you wear at the hospital are not the same. Kind of like an education awareness for condoms is needed.

The second thing is that this is more expensive for people. It is not feasible for everyone to have air filters in their homes. My home for example has an air filter in every room in our house and a portable pollution monitor to ensure that they are cleaning out air enough. The best we can do is get the air down to 35 or 50. Make sure homes are sealed and do not let outside air in.

Of course, this is important with schools as well. Schools need to get air filters in their rooms. Schools in China need to budget for air filters.

Rein: Do you see a shift in how Chinese define the aspirational lifestyle?

Liu: JUCCCE's China Dream initiative is really about visualizing how the 900 million urban residents that China will have by 2030 can live dignified and vibrant lives in this dense urban landscape. This is the first time in world history where you have so many people living in such crowded quarters.

We need innovation on the urban landscape, which allows us to use fewer resources and to balance or lessen people's impact on the world. A fundamental problem is that right now today China's per capita disposable income is one-tenth of Americans'. In 2000 it was one-twenty-fourth. So we are rapidly closing gap on disposable income. If every single person views the image of American success, like *Gossip Girl* or [the Chinese film] *Tiny Times,* then we are going to run into big problems because the world cannot support creating that much material for that kind of demand. What people do not realize is that a lot of Americans, like Hollywood actors, are not trying to pursue a *Gossip Girl*–style lifestyle but are focusing more on experience, memories, and interactions on getting closer with friends and family rather than accumulating stuff, like buying a hundred Birkin bags. They might be surprised to know for example that Leonardo DiCaprio owns electric cars, or Ben Affleck shops for vegan food in Whole Foods.

The China Dream initiative is drawing a compelling picture that creates a dignified lifestyle that is rooted in Chinese values that are more sustainable and lets us live in a dense urban landscape.

The key thing JUCCCE is trying to teach primary kids especially is how they fit in an ecosystem. There are two things they need to learn about: (1) respecting other people and respecting the ecosystem and (2) understanding the supply chain of things, the circular economy, and the food chain. If more people understand that an action or a decision they make will impact an entire chain of events that will impact the earth, they will think about each action they take more carefully.

For example what JUCCCE is doing. In February 2013 we launched a program called "A New Way to Eat." People were saying nutrition needs to come together with sustainable agriculture. We created curriculum that we are piloting in Y. K. Pao (founded by Hong Kong shipping magnate and philanthropist Y. K. Pao). Teaching primary school kids how to eat in a way that is good for them and for the planet.

We teach 45-minute classes and work with local chefs for (British catering services company) Compass, which cooks yummy and healthier school lunches. In the past we had just translated American food pyramid, which is not that healthy—it was pushed by food lobbyists. We are moving more toward Michelle Obama's My Plate initiative. China has a growing problem with how we are eating. Fifty percent of Chinese are prediabetic. Twelve percent have type 1 diabetes. It's an astounding fact, and it's because we have been overwhelmed by fast food chains, such as KFC, Baskin Robbins, Pizza Hut, McDonald's, and Dunkin' Donuts. We need to teach kids how to eat in a way that is healthier for them and allow them to fuel their mind and body to be more focused in school.

If we are going to have 9.2 billion people on Earth and eat as we do, we will not have enough arable land for beef. We are going to lose commercially viable fish by 2050 if we keep eating and fishing the way we are today. We do not have enough arable land globally to feed rising meat consumption that is happening in China. Rising disposable income means people eat more meat. Beef more than anything needs more arable land and more water and more fertilizer than pollutes the soil, energy to transport. Fifty percent of food is wasted before it even hits our plates because of inefficiency in the supply chain.

Pollution Is Changing Where and How People Shop

The rising attention paid to air pollution is hitting China's department stores three times over. First, consumers are reallocating their budgets away from the midtier products sold in most department stores and are instead spending money on experiences, such as overseas tourism.

Second, on polluted days, consumers try to minimize the amount of time they have to spend outside and look for places to go and shop where they can spend a full day. Department stores in China tend to be smaller than malls and can be covered in the space of an hour or two, not enough for a full-day outing. Meanwhile, developers, such as CapitaLand from Singapore, or Hong Kong's Sun Hung Kai Properties, are building huge malls with enough different amenities to cover a full-day spree—shops, cafés, parking lots, movie theaters, and restaurants—all under one roof. Consumers are driving to malls where they can park underground, shop, and eat without ever setting foot outdoors in the toxic air.

Third, rising e-commerce websites VIPshop and Yihaodian not only allow the comfort of shopping from home but also trump department stores in terms of selection and low prices. Overall, department stores will face challenges in the coming five years and will have to embark on major changes to their product selection and site location strategies.

Key Action Item: Brands need to develop sales channels and marketing strategies that take into account the shifts that air pollution problems are accelerating. Outdoor events and pop-up stores will underperform if pollution levels are bad on the day of the initiative, because most people will check not only the skies but also the air quality readings on their smartphone apps. Instead, choose locations such as malls or launch e-commerce initiatives, especially ones that work well on mobile devices, which will do well regardless of pollution.

Premium Antipollution Products

Consumers are so concerned about air pollution that they are spending on the most high-tech air-filtering products they can afford. They refuse to go cheap because they feel this is literally a life-or-death purchase. High-end air and water purifier brands, such as Blu Air or 3M, as well as masks from Vogmask (and 3M) are selling very well.

Companies need to focus on supply chain because many products are sold out and on back order. When a bad air day hits, companies need to be prepared for a sharp spike in demand. They also need to pay attention to appearance—many air purifiers on the market do not appear to have been designed with style in mind. Large air purifier units are harder to ignore because many homes are small and they are put in every room. Consumers do not want to fill their apartments with ugly, boxy machines.

Key Action Item: Emphasize well-designed antipollution products with top-of-the-line technology. Consumers do not want functional but ugly appliances because they are so noticeable in homes. Home decoration is one of the fastest-growing segments, and antipollution products need to fit into the design schemes of home owners and interior designers.

Similarly, masks must both be comfortable and have attractive designs, both for women (a mix of chic and cute) and for children (focus on fun and popular cartoon characters) because kids often take masks off if they don't like the way they look. Different design choices for masks are vital, because consumers view them as fashion items where they can display uniqueness in the choice of their design.

6

THE END OF BLING

I t sounds like a ridiculous problem to have," Mr. Chen told me one hazy day in Beijing as we zoomed around in his red Ferrari, "but I don't know where to spend my money." Originally, Chen had made his money in real estate in Hainan Island in the late 1980s and early 1990s before moving to Beijing, where he cultivated the connections needed to do "big real estate projects." By the time we had become friendly, Chen had become one of the country's largest developers, with commercial and residential developments spanning the country.

In the past Chen had typically parked his money in his own developments but was expecting lower returns in real estate, so he was taking money out of property investments and wondering what to do with it. He considered investing in real estate developments in America or buying homes in Maui and New York, but he only travels there once or twice yearly, usually to visit his daughter, who is attending an elite New England boarding school.

"I used to buy the newest and best car from every luxury brand," he told me. I've seen them—in his garage at his palatial home in

Beijing, he houses Porsches, Range Rovers, and a mini fleet of S600 Mercedes. But, he continued, "I haven't bought a new car in over a year." Despite his political connections and wealth, Mr. Chen also hasn't even been able to obtain a license plate in Beijing for the past year. Under new restrictions to keep the number of cars down, Beijingers now have to apply for license plates in monthly auctions; fewer than 1 percent of applicants actually secure one.

Restrictions on home buying and automobiles are hitting China's billionaires and forcing a reallocation of spending. Municipal governments around the country have implemented restrictions on license plates to reduce traffic congestion and pollution. As the founder and chief executive officer (CEO) of the New York Stock Exchange–listed (NYSE) Bitauto, Li Bin, told me, "After Shanghai and Beijing, other cities like Guangzhou, Tianjin, and Hangzhou also introduced restriction measures. Because the rapid growth of automobiles was not anticipated during urban planning, traffic congestion has become a serious problem in large cities in China, and it will take a long time to resolve."

Li thinks the regulations will continue to spread throughout the country. "Additional large cities with high rates of car adoption may introduce restriction measures to curb congestion as well." Real estate restrictions, put in place because of concerns about speculation, are also changing purchasing patterns.

Chen told me in 2014 he has no place to invest his money. "I don't trust the stock market—there's too much fraud and manipulation."

As we turned onto the 3rd Ring Road, I asked Chen what he is doing with his money. He said he was currently building a sprawling 2,000-square-meter mansion in Beijing, with "the best of everything imported from everywhere. Marble and curtains from Italy. Teakwood from Myanmar." All told, he estimated he was spending about $50 million.

Limits on the number of homes individuals can buy have created demand for megamansions. Five years ago, few homes sold for more than $5 to $10 million. Now, new complexes with $15 million homes, some at $80 to $100 million at 20,000 to 30,000 square meters, no, it is saying total price of $80 to $100 million and price per square meter of $20,000-$30,000 are becoming common.

Instead of buying multiple homes to flip, home buyers are purchasing a single home to live in and spending small fortunes to renovate and decorate them.

Most of these multimillion-dollar mansions look pretty much the same on the outside, but the reality is actually different once you go inside. Unlike in America where most home buyers can choose from preselected interiors, including flooring and walls, in China most homes are sold as empty concrete shells. Home buyers have to choose and install wiring, floors, lights, and even pipes.

The ultrawealthy used to copy others and deck out in the same gaudy faux–Louis XIV style with the same gilded molding and leopard print upholstery, but the trend toward uniqueness in home decoration is emerging because people are now familiar with the decoration process, having renovated homes before.

Intentionally decorating his house differently from everyone around him, Chen told me is adorning his home with fixtures, furniture, and other decorative items he buys on trips around the world to create "a warm, homey feel that my wife likes, different from everyone else." He bought carpets made from animal hides while on safari trips to South Africa. He is hanging ebony wood carvings from his trips to Indonesia and Thailand.

Limits on home and car purchases combined with capital controls mean there are fewer big-ticket items China's wealthy can buy inside the country. Prohibited from buying multiple vacation homes, as rich New Yorkers do in the Hamptons or Bostonians do in Nantucket, wealthy Chinese put more money into main homes.

Fortunes are being spent on artwork, furniture, and home decoration. Poly Culture, an offshoot of the largest state-owned developer, Poly Group, specializing in antique collection and artwork auctions, saw its stock price soar in its initial public offering in 2014 because investors know wealthy people are buying art, partially to show sophistication and investment but also because they do not know where else to put their money. Chinese became the world's largest buyers of artwork in 2013, with purchases exceeding $4 billion.

Chen is also buying cut and uncut diamonds to fashion custom-made jewelry for relatives. He thinks it is "distinctive and nice" to make jewelry because the result is more unique than buying store-bought jewelry brands from big fashion houses.

Some spending by wealthy Chinese is going offshore, often through somewhat dubious means in Macau by falsely buying products via UnionPay, a domestic Chinese bank card organization that competes with Visa and Mastercard. Consumers buy products via UnionPay, then return items less a commission to get around convertibility limits. For instance, they might buy a $200,000 watch with their UnionPay card, then return it for $190,000 in cash while the store pockets a 5 percent commission. Others use illegal money changers, *Huangniu,* that slink near banks and popular tourist spots.

When traveling abroad, China's wealthy are skipping the well-trod path to Paris and Rome and venturing to ever more exotic locales, such as South Africa or Alaska, according to interviews China Market Research Group (CMR) conducted with a dozen billionaires. China's truly wealthy are looking to be different from everyone else.

Billionaires are also spending more money on big-ticket items, such as jets and yachts, where few restrictions exist. In recent years, the military has opened up airspace to accommodate private jets, and domestic Chinese airports have started to rent out hangars for private aircraft to park. General Dynamics' Gulfstream Aerospace is doing a resounding business selling to Chinese.

☙

Buying a thousand-dollar Louis Vuitton (LV) or Gucci handbag in the 1990s was a dream most Chinese never thought they could achieve, like buying a quarter-million-dollar Ferrari or Rolls-Royce for most Americans today. Foreign brands, even mass-market ones, such as Prell shampoo or Nike sneakers, represented success. Consumers bought counterfeit clothes and knockoff bags plastered with fake Ralph Lauren and Prada logos at markets, such as Silk Street in Beijing or Xiangyang Market in Shanghai, as a function of poverty rather than from any lack of morality. The wealthiest gained prestige from toting the right handbag.

Luxury items remained out of the reach of many by the turn of the millennium. Conspicuous consumption and showing off bling became integral to gaining social status. Handbags, pens, and watches with easily recognizable logos from brands such as LV, Omega, and Mont Blanc flew off the racks. The bigger, louder, and more in your face the logo was, the better.

By the late 2000s, Chinese had become the new Japanese of the 1980s. Chinese accounted for about 20 percent of worldwide luxury goods by 2012 and crowded boutiques along Fifth Avenue in New York and the Champs-Élysées in Paris. Luxury retailers hired Mandarin-speaking sales clerks.

Bling still reigned supreme. Middle-class consumers purchased LV and Prada apparel in droves; by 2013 consumers there accounted for 50 percent of LV's global sales. By this point these objects were now officially for the mainstream—and therefore no longer desirable to the truly wealthy. One wealthy Chinese woman from Beijing told me she would not buy anything from LV because it was "too common"—even office secretaries making $800 a month were saving up, often by skipping lunch, to buy LV-print polyvinyl chloride (PVC) handbags.

Billionaires switched to more exclusive brands, such as Chanel, Bottega Veneta, and Hermès, and started focusing on acquiring bigger-ticket items, such as cars. The nation in 2014 became the largest market for Porsche and Rolls-Royce. Wealthy consumers bought private jets and high-end wines, and started sending their children to the top boarding schools, such as St. Paul's and Andover in the United States.

To find out more about the shopping habits of China's ultra-wealthy, I interviewed Marty Wikstrom in 2014. Wikstrom headed the fashion and accessories division of Compagnie Financière Richemont, the world's second-largest luxury goods holding company, from 2009 to 2013 as CEO and now serves as the chair of Harrys of London, one of the finest purveyors of handmade shoes with rubber soles that has emerged as the go-to brand for the young royals, counting Princess Beatrice, the Duchess of Westminster, and Tom Parker Bowles as clients.

I'd met with her in Paris and Shanghai over the past several years and always found she had her finger on the pulse of the lifestyles of China's rich and famous.

"The Chinese consumer is becoming much more discerning in their taste level and spending habits," Wikstrom told me. Her Harrys of London brand is a prime example. Worn by Emmy-winning English actor Damian Lewis for his upcoming film, Harrys' shoes are among the world's most exclusive—they sell from several hundred to several thousand British pounds per pair and are increasingly popular among wealthy Chinese visiting

London. These customers value "craftsmanship, materials, heritage, and durability," she said, and these priorities "are evolving to trump conspicuous consumption and labels as key criteria for purchases."

"But isn't buying to achieve social status still important?" I asked.

"While status remains integral to the culture, there has been an evident shift in purchasing in order to develop one's own individual and unique style," Wikstrom answered. In her view this shift "has no doubt been accelerated by the government's anti-corruption campaign" since 2012, "coupled with a global shift away from logos and the general decline in overt consumption" since the financial crisis in 2008.

Overt logo-heavy brands, such as LV, have fallen out of favor not because of evolving tastes and sophistication but only out of a desire to stand out less.

Wikstrom referred to this as the "stealth wealth" movement; to be less conspicuous and differentiate from their peers, the affluent are seeking out lower-profile niche brands, such as Harrys of London, and multibrand boutiques, such as Brioni or Kiton. Wikstrom said this also creates an opening for Chinese brands, such as domestic Chinese brand Exception, which the first lady was seen toting to Moscow on her first official state visit, "which many knowledgeable consumers are starting to rate over certain Western brands in select categories," such as handbags and outerwear.

"What are ultrawealthy looking for now?" I asked.

Wikstrom answered, "Savvy Chinese shoppers are now targeting brands which offer a point of differentiation that reflects their own sophisticated style and maturing outlook: superior customer experience, bespoke and exclusive pieces, and products with intrinsic value."

Wikstrom's analysis mirrors the experience that Richard Schaeffer, the owner of Cape Cobra, a South African maker of premium animal hide products for brands such as Tiffany's, Michael Kors, and Chloé. Schaeffer told me that his branded crocodile and ostrich leather goods were selling so well to Chinese stopping by his boutiques in Cape Town who typically spend at the "extreme high end of society." He had also signed a deal with the Sparkle Roll Group Limited to sell ostrich goods in Beijing starting in 2013, because Chinese desire different and more exclusive brands. Sales have outpaced their initial projects by multitudes.

⬥

"I just bought a Gulfstream 550," Mr. Ye told me as we dined at his swanky private club. Ye is one of China's richest men but maintains an extremely low profile—he does not appear on any China rich list like those from *Hurun* or *Forbes,* although he would certainly qualify, and has never done an interview with a media publication. Better not to stand out too much, as he put it to me. He would only speak to me because he trusted me not to do anything to harm him.

Jade figurines and ancient steel bells adorned the walls of the club. Ye pointed at a few he called priceless. Ye's wife had a Chanel bag and a matching pink suit and black pumps. Ye wore a modern version of the Sun Yat-Sen collar shirt. Often traveling to Yemen and other Middle Eastern and African countries for energy deals, he said owning a private jet has been a lifesaver.

Private jet sales are soaring, leading many firms to sell their first jets to Chinese buyers rather than to Middle Eastern royalty as before. Yachting is also becoming popular, with housing com-plexes on Hainan Island touting private moors. The corruption crackdown has affected yacht sales but mostly sales to corporations. The number of brands that exhibited at the Hainan Rendez-Vous in 2014 dropped to 72, down from 139 the year before. But yacht sales to wealthy individuals are continuing to show impressive gains, a yacht maker told me. The market still has much room to grow, if China were to hit similar per capita purchases of yachts as Hong Kong, where one in 25 wealthy Chinese is a yacht owner, compared with one out of every 318 mainlander, according to the Italian Trade Commission.[1]

⮒⮒⮒

Despite changing tastes and the desire to maintain a lower profile, luxury items remain important in China—the underlying drivers for buying them are changing, as is the focus on certain and product categories, but overall spending remains strong.

In 2006 CMR undertook research for a Hong Kong–based luxury retailer, Asia's equivalent of a Saks Fifth Avenue or Neiman Marcus. One of the key findings revealed consumers all wanted the same five to 10 brands—LV, Ermenegildo Zegna, Dunhill, and only a few others. Buying the same brands let them display they achieved being part of the in crowd, but fear drove a large part of decision making. Consumers worried about buying the wrong label and looking stupid and unsophisticated. It was almost like high school all over again.

When CMR conducted exit interviews with men shopping at suit maker Zegna, many told us they simply bought whatever draped on the mannequin—the suit, the tie, the shirt, the belt, the shoes, everything—because they wanted to look the right way. They did not know how to mix and match.

Zegna ran ad campaigns in 2006 with taglines such as "Great men think alike." That message simply won't fly anymore in a market where consumers increasingly feel confident enough to think and decide for themselves.

An emerging class of well-to-do white-collar employees is also boosting demand for premium brands, such as Michael Kors and Coach, positioned just below mass luxury brands, such as LV. White collars are starting to think they will never be truly wealthy, a major change from five years ago when many believed they were on their way to riches.

In 2009, when CMR interviewed middle-class Chinese in tier-one cities, such as Shanghai, most felt they were still on their way to true riches. CMR research in 2013 showed sentiment has changed dramatically—most reported feeling like they would never get ultrarich because they missed out on the real estate boom of the previous decade.

With their aim slightly lower than in the past, middle-class consumers are trading down from aspiration brands to ones positioned lower on the prestige scale, from LV to Burberry, Max Mara, and Tory Burch. The wealthiest consumers, on the other hand, are trading up to Chanel and Hermès, leaving mass luxury brands, such as Gucci, Prada, and LV, alone in the middle.

⟨⟨⟩⟩

President Xi Jinping's far-reaching crackdown on corruption spurred a shift in which luxury brands and categories are popular and stalled overall growth. Luxury sales growth plummeted from 30 percent in 2011 to 7 percent in 2012 to just 2 percent in 2013. Observing this drop, Merryn Somerset Webb of *MoneyWeek* concluded in an op-ed for the *Financial Times* in August 2013 the anticorruption campaign will destroy the sales of luxury brands across the board and all categories. According to this view, which other analysts share, the use of luxury goods as illegal gifts by corrupt businesspeople and officials was what was propping up sales growth for luxury. But is that really true?

A more nuanced picture of the role of gifting in the luxury sector than Somerset's indicates a different view. Gifting accounts for only 20 percent of luxury product purchases for most brands in China. This percentage skews much higher for certain specific categories most closely associated with under-the-table gifts, such as high-end tea, watches, alcohol, and high-end cigarettes. There are also differences by brands—LV and Omega have traditionally been more popular brands to gift than apparel brands such as Yves Saint Laurent or Max Mara. There are also stark differences by gender, with men's products far more exposed to illegal gifting than women's accessories and apparel.

Based on research CMR conducted in 2012 and 2013 with 1,000 buyers of luxury items, we found that of the 20 percent of typical revenues that come from gifting, half (i.e., 10 percent of overall sales) is to friends. The government crackdown will not affect this business as much as some believe. Of the remaining 50 percent of gifting sales, 50 percent of that (or 5 percent of overall sales) is business-to-business gifting. The remaining 50 percent (5 percent of overall sales) is corrupt gifting to government officials. For most brands here not that much money is being given to officials in bribes.

What is a far more serious threat to brands is when government officials use state budgets to buy luxury items and for spending. Many officials have below-market-average salaries for people in their standing. It is common for officials to make less than $1,000 a month. They have been using their budgets to buy gifts for other officials.

Sales of high-end teas, such as the famous *longjing* green tea, are down 70 percent from previous years, and several thousand high-end restaurants went out of business in 2013 alone. More than 50 five-star hotels lobbied to lose a star as the government implemented regulations on officials against staying in five-star hotels and flying business class. The government has also reduced the number of nights officials can stay in hotels and shortened the duration and number of overseas trips.

The regulatory environment combined with increased sophistication is changing the landscape of luxury buying by wealthy Chinese. They are shifting toward buying to attain a lifestyle they aspire to, often rooted in Chinese nationalism, rather than to show off their wealth and status. Equally clear is that many brands in the luxury sector still have ample opportunities for growth.

Gareth Incledon, Managing Director, HUGO BOSS China

Before moving into the fashion world, Gareth Incledon spent 12 years in the British army and is a qualified chartered management accountant. He joined HUGO BOSS from Sixty UK Ltd. (Miss Sixty) in 2005 as finance director. He moved to Denmark in 2009 as managing director, responsible for HUGO BOSS Nordic, before moving to Shanghai as managing director, responsible for HUGO BOSS China retail in 2012. He has a wife and two boys. He used to play rugby and is now coaching kids in Shanghai. I first met Incledon soon after he arrived in Shanghai.

Rein: HUGO BOSS has performed better than most brands during the slowdown of the luxury sector in the wake of the anticorruption campaign. What have you done to maintain your edge?

Incledon: There is no doubt that President Xi Jinping's crackdown has had an effect on the luxury-goods market and the purchasing of ostentatious luxury items on the mainland at least. Leather goods, accessories, and watches were arguably some of the most desirable product groups within the fashion sector. Whilst leather goods, accessories, and watches form a key element of the offer of any lifestyle brand, these product groups have traditionally played a less significant role in our business. Neither have we relied on iconic patterns and products or overt logotypes, choosing to concentrate instead on discreet and discerning marks of quality to ensure success. A combination of these factors along with a greater reliance on personal consumption has meant that HUGO BOSS, whilst being far from immune to the effects of the slowdown has fared relatively well during this period of austerity and change.

We have retained its general price position whilst developing our product offer in both entry- and luxury-price segments. Whilst pricing strategy is, and will continue to remain key, we also see great opportunity in being able to develop the width of price value of products and lines we are able to offer the Chinese market from our already comprehensive collection base. The expansion of our women's wear offer, driven by the recent recruitment of the outstanding creative talent of Jason Wu, is an important factor in achieving a broader brand appeal.

The recent opening of flagship stores in Shanghai and Hong Kong will not only allow us to showcase a wider assortment to our consumers but also give us the opportunity to introduce permanent value-added luxury services such as our BOSS Made to Measure tailor service. We intend, over time, to provide these services and assortment on an appropriate scale in many of the other key cities such as Beijing, Shenzhen, and Chengdu. These investments can also be rightly seen as an indicator of the brand's longer-term commitment to developing our retail business in the greater China market as a whole.

Rein: What role does gifting play in China in the luxury sector versus individual consumption?

Incledon: Despite the near eradication of gifting for official government purposes, I believe that, whilst the typical ticket price is likely to be much lower, the practice of giving gifts will continue to blossom from a general market perspective. It will play an important part in driving the personal consumption needed by luxury-goods brands to fill the void left by the demise of official practice. And so in the future I believe there will remain two significant channels for gifting.

Firstly, and probably of greater importance, giving gifts to one another is an affectionate courtesy deeply embedded in Chinese culture. The traditional opportunities surrounding festivals and family events already exist and continue to flourish. However, the addition of more commercially driven reasons and opportunities to give gifts such as Valentine's Day and Single's Day will undoubtedly see gifting remain and in all likelihood begin to grow again in significance for many brands in the future.

Secondly, as the Chinese luxury and consumer market matures its segmentation will force retailers to focus not only on attracting new consumers but also on how to retain and reward loyal customers. The development of customer relationship marketing tools [presents an] opportunity for brands from different segments and markets to cooperate to provide rewards to loyal consumers attractive to their diverse consumption desires and aspirations.

Rein: Do you see men or women taking up a larger percentage of luxury sales?

Incledon: Until recently the Chinese luxury market ran opposite every other major luxury market in the world in that it was male-dominated. The balance has already been redressed to an estimated 50-50 split in 2013 according to Bain. But the European market by comparison is at 35-65 split in favor of women, so there is every reason to believe that the strong evidence of growth in female consumption in China will continue for the foreseeable future. There are many factors influencing this growth but rapidly changing social attitudes and the high participation of females in the workplace will undoubtedly support the midterm rise in female consumption. Whilst menswear will continue to contribute the lion's share of our future revenues the percentage share of women's wear will increase from what we see today and will be proportionally our strongest growth area.

Rein: Chinese are traveling abroad more and more. What opportunities and challenges arise from this?

Incledon: Chinese nationals are not only traveling abroad in greater numbers and frequency but are also purchasing an increasing amount of their luxury items outside of mainland China. In 2013 Bain estimated this phenomenon as being 67 percent of all purchases made by mainland Chinese. This trend, whilst creating volatility in the domestic market, provides brands with a unique opportunity for their global distribution to benefit and indeed participate in the substantial investments made in developing brand equity in China.

Price is a key motivation for buying outside of mainland China, but by no means the only consideration. Levels of service and authenticity of buying brands in their home market are also key deciding factors. And whilst the consumer can journey around the globe with relative ease, their expectation and perception of the brand if not ideally enhanced should at least be sustained along the way if not ideally enhanced.

We fully recognize this reasonable expectation placed on us by our loyal consumers and have implemented strategies such as the rapid expansion of our own global retail network have given us to control the experience our consumers receive when entering one of our stores, be it in Shanghai, Hong Kong, or Paris. Global standards in product presentation, staff training—including the placement of Mandarin-speaking staff in many global key stores to assist our Chinese consumers—modern, consistent, and exciting store design will ensure that our customer's expectations and needs can be met wherever he or she decides to shop. We are also looking at ways of sharing information on consumer buying behavior between regions with a view to refining our product offer to meet specific tastes such as style and color and enhancing the accessibility of customer services such as tailoring and returns. I believe that as a principle we should cater not just to the needs of the China market but to the requirements of the Chinese consumers wherever they may visit and shop.

Rein: According to the Hurun Report, HUGO BOSS's women's collections are now a top 10 desirable fashion brands despite being traditionally known in China for men's collections. How did you achieve this success?

Incledon: HUGO BOSS has an established and successful women's wear business in many key markets throughout the world. For historic reasons, mainly associated with the prevailing market conditions for luxury products in China, we have until recently decided not to fully represent and distribute our women's wear products in the market.

However, whilst HUGO BOSS featured again amongst the top two men's luxury fashion brands in China, it is true that in the 2013 Hurun survey of high-net-worth individuals in China saw our women's wear brand feature in the top 10 most desirable fashion brands for the first time. Many events took place in 2013 that served to promote our BOSS women's wear brand; 70 percent of the styles featured in our Shanghai fashion show in May 2013 were from our women's collection; the summer saw the outstanding talents of Jason Wu added to our team as creative director for BOSS woman's wear; the autumn saw the opening of our Shanghai flagship stores with new flagship stores in Hong Kong also opening before Chinese New Year. All stores proudly present an extensive assortment of our latest women's wear collection. Overseas travel is certainly another factor; significant presentation of our women's wear can be seen in all our global key stores generating awareness of our products as well as opportunity to buy.

Whilst the significant expansion of women's wear is still to come in China, limited distribution to date has provided us with some valuable insight as to the subtle differences attributable to the Chinese consumer. Such knowledge has allowed us to make innovations such as adapting our general fit scaling to be more accommodating to the Asian silhouette. This is also in fact true of many of our menswear product categories but we found these requirements even more profound when considering the women's wear need. We have also noted for example a difference in taste for colors and patterns. These learnings are not only being incorporated into our buying methodology but are also incorporated by our creative team at an early stage of the collection design to ensure we cater for the needs of the China market.

Rein: What is your view on changes in the retail sector, such as falling department store sales and the rise of e-commerce?

Incledon: For the political, social, economic reasons mentioned earlier, customer traffic to individual points of sale has fallen in the last 18 months. This has affected both department stores and malls and is also further accentuated by a significant proliferation of available retail space over the last three years or so. But whether they are affected equally is dependent on a wide range of factors. However, there were certainly certain advantages to operating in department stores. They tended to be more established, offered a broader product range and had often developed superior retail and customer service knowledge whilst adopting a more retail-minded approach. This expertise was typically in need of development within mall operations.

There is evidence, however, that malls are changing their approach, so the challenge for department stores will be to evolve and update their shopping environment and product offer to meet the changing needs of the consumer. This will be no easy task as malls in China are typically large enough to offer a critical mass of brand and product offer along with numerous lifestyle options in areas such as food and beverage, cinemas, etc. Therefore in the long term, I believe the consumer preference for malls will continue and sales will develop accordingly. I'm sure the emergence of the "third" way of malls with stand-alone stores anchored by a department store will grow in popularity with a broad range of consumers in major population centers. In these cities I see malls in the future offering a better opportunity and competitor environment for our main BOSS brand and thus accounting for an increasing share of revenues. But by their very nature of presenting a wide variety of brands by category I believe that quality department stores will still present a good opportunity for the development of diffusion or secondary lifestyle brands.

The opportunities offered by e-commerce in China are truly staggering. The use of digital and mobile technology is vast and continues to grow. HUGO BOSS successfully opened its China e-commerce store in 2013. We choose to operate the store ourselves and not use a store run by a third party. One of the key reasons to being a pioneer in this regard was the acknowledgment that service, be it interactive online product advice and help or quality of logistical support, is a crucial component of our brand value. We believe that by directly managing the operation of our ecommerce store, in close cooperation with an established fulfillment partner, we can ensure the highest level of customer service and care to our consumers.

This achieved, there is no doubting that when making valuable purchases consumers will still like to enjoy the levels of service and experience the ambiance provided by our stand-alone stores. But I would rather not see the future as off-line and online commerce being mutually exclusive. I see almost unquantifiable opportunity in an omnichannel approach where all the touch points between the brand and consumer are integrated using both traditional and digital mediums of communication and commerce.

Rein: Many brands like Louis Vuitton have decided to refocus on first-tier cities like Shanghai and Beijing. Do you believe the great growth is going to come from tier 1 cities or do you think it makes sense to have more sales points in third- to fifth-tier cities?

Incledon: There is of course a much higher proportion of wealth in tier-one and -two cities. This will no doubt continue to grow and so it would seem natural for luxury brands to be concentrated in this environment. Lower-tier cities in most countries often look to larger cities for a lead in trends, so a strong presence in tier-one and -two cities is key to maintaining and enhancing the brand equity needed to underpin any successful strategy implemented in other cities. HUGO BOSS has fully recognized and addressed this requirement with the opening of flagship stores and the systematic upgrading of other stores in the many of the provincial capitals.

However, according to a recent study by McKinsey the percentage of middle-class families and their relative wealth in the third- and fourth-tier cities is expected to grow from just 18 percent in 2002 to nearly 40 percent in 2022. This upper middle class will account for nearly 55 percent of urban consumption as opposed to 20 percent in 2002. This rate of growth in third- and fourth-tier cities over the next seven years or so makes those cities an attractive proposition for entry-level luxury brands such as HUGO BOSS. It is also worth considering that whilst tier-one and -two cities harbor the relative wealth it could be argued that they are also the most vulnerable at present to the effects of political changes and international travel. They also face in the short term at least greater degrees of competition from multiple industries aiming to provide greater lifestyle choices for consumers to enjoy their wealth.

What I believe is certain is that as the market matures it will provide multiple niches in which brands will position themselves.

Rein: To what extent do you see a sense of individualism emerging? What changes do you see in consumer aspirations and how is HUGO BOSS catering to that change?

Incledon: There is little doubt that the Chinese consumer is becoming ever more discerning. I believe the degree to which people seek true or extreme individualism is influenced by the cultural norms within society and it is difficult to judge how far this will develop in China at present. What is evident by the rapid expansion of a diverse business offer in China is that the appetite of the Chinese consumer to experience new things be it fashion, technology, or travel but to name a few appears almost inexhaustible. This phenomenon will inevitably provide opportunities for new brands and products to challenge the established order of luxury players in the market. This in my opinion can only be a positive and healthy occurrence for both the brands and the consumer.

The End of Bling: The Rise of Niche Brands

China's wealthiest consumers are moving away from buying clothing and shoes to broadcast their wealth to buying exclusive, discreet niche brands that fit their lifestyle aspirations. Chanel, Bottega Veneta, and Hermès bags are popular, and most consumers know they are so exclusive because of their high price tags and more refined, subtle design cues, such as Bottega Veneta's woven leather and Chanel's minimalism rather than bold, flashy designs with big logos.

Going forward, the trend will move toward even higher-priced niche brands with strong heritage, with which buyers can display individuality, such as men's shoe company Harrys of London, where most pairs of shoes cost 300 to 500 British pounds. The company has seen soaring sales to Chinese men traveling to London looking for something distinctive but of the absolute finest workmanship.

Another example would be Shanghai Tang, which has fast become popular among Chinese by understanding the rising pride in Chinese luxury brands. As Sylvain Rocher, director, digital business development and customer relationship management, told me, "Chinese want something that they can enjoy every day of their busy lives, with some subtle and elegant references to China." As a result, the brand has changed its styles to refine its "product offering in an attempt to reconcile fashion and modernity with personal and intimate Chinese codes."

Key Action Item: Limit supply of products and sales points, focus on specific consumer niches, and use artistry that counterfeiters cannot easily replicate, as Harrys of London and Shanghai Tang have done.

Armani for instance has had issues with knockoffs in China—Giorgio Armani himself said he could not tell the difference between counterfeit Armani watches and the real thing. Similarly, the Gucci canvas bag is easily counterfeited. Markets that sell pirated goods have three tiers of counterfeit items: cheap domestic knockoffs, better-quality domestic fakes, and high-end counterfeits from South Korea. It can be very hard to tell the difference between real and Korean counterfeit pirated items for a canvas or PVC bag.

This is different from high-end leather handbags, such as the Birkin from Hermès or the cross-stitching from Bottega Veneta, that maintain exclusivity with fewer sales points. The distinctive and high-quality artistry is also less likely to be copycatted.

Immigration and Capital Flight

Growing unease marks the life of many of China's wealthiest. The corruption crackdown Xi Jinping launched in 2012 is very real, catching many wealthy and their political patrons in dragnets.

Worried about getting arrested, many are immigrating abroad and taking money offshore. In many cases the person will stay in China for business while his or her family will move abroad. Areas with little pollution where there are a lot of outdoor activities are popular, such as Sydney, Vancouver,

Seattle, and California. There also need to be good education opportunities nearby as well as easy transportation back to China. This is a great opportunity for real estate and immigration lawyers. By 2014, *Reuters* found that Chinese had replaced Russians to become the most frequent buyers of real estate in Manhattan.

Key Action Items: Selling to the Chinese consumer no longer means selling just into China. Brands need to create global Chinese consumer strategies and be ready to sell to them when they travel abroad. For instance, one of the world's largest hotel chains engaged my firm to develop a Chinese consumer strategy because they found so many Chinese were guests in far-off properties throughout Europe and Asia.

Enrichment and Education

The new status symbol among China's elite is to get their children into the top American boarding schools, such as St. Paul's and Exeter. U.K. schools, such as Eton and Harrow, are popular, too, but not as popular as American schools because Chinese parents view America and China as the new world economic superpowers and want networking opportunities for their children.

Even middle-class Chinese are spending lots of money on brands that can help enrich children and make them more competitive to get into schools that are soaring. After school and summer activities for children, such as art and music classes, are in high demand. Primary school kids are being sent to learn English in America, Australia, and even Bali during vacation.

Key Action Item: Brands that position themselves as benefiting children's competitiveness will do well. Competition in China to get into top schools is so fierce that even the wealthiest families are concerned about the futures of their children. Parents are buying everything from ergonomic chairs and study lights to mechanical pencils to help children study better as well as music and painting lessons to help children's minds develop.

7

CHINA'S
EXPANDING
CONSUMER CLASS

Her face had the excited flush of imminent motherhood as
she opened the door. "Welcome to my home," the
27-year-old Vanessa Zhu beamed. She handed us disposable
slippers saved from some hotel trip. The lingering scent of spicy
Sichuan food from last night's dinner hung in the air.

Accompanying me was Maureen, the chief operating officer of
one of the world's largest consumer goods companies. We were
in the middle of a six-month project translating insights from
home visits and in-depth interviews into new products and
packaging designs.

The first home we visited was Vanessa's in a newer section of
Chengdu, the capital of Sichuan province, famed for its fash-
ionable women and a laid-back tea culture. Vanessa's husband,
Xiao Wen, was off at his $800-a-month job as a sales executive in

a multinational firm, so Vanessa was showing us through their home.

A sheen of sweat beaded up on Vanessa's forehead as she waddled through her two-bedroom, 70-square-meter (approximately 700-square-foot) home. Although she had a Haier air conditioner unit installed, it was turned off. She told us she usually had it switched off and other electric appliances unplugged "to save on electricity costs."

Vanessa spent most of her time preparing for her baby's arrival. Family and friends had bought gender-neutral items for the baby, because nobody knew whether it would be a boy or a girl. The government prohibited doctors from telling expectant parents the gender of their baby before birth because of fears that families limited to only one child will favor boys and seek abortions if they know they are going to have a girl. China has a skewed sex ratio, with 118 boys born per 100 girls, according to the 2010 census. The typical biological rate should be 103 to 107, according to the National Bureau of Statistics.

Vanessa explained she and Xiao Wen worried about the toxicity in paint and furniture, so they had already painted the walls with Nippon Paint, a trusted Japanese brand, and bought the crib from Goodbaby, a Chinese maker of baby products with a good reputation for safety. They had also bought wooden dressers far in advance so that all the furniture, paint, and curtains could air out formaldehyde and other toxic smells.

Most Chinese home buyers buy everything new when they move into a new home, from curtains to dressers made from compounded wood to tables. There are few hand-me-downs and most consider older furniture garbage rather than antiques. The mix of smells from all the new items can get overpowering.

Foreign-branded diapers and cans of baby formula stacked nearly to the ceiling crowded a corner of the baby's room. Storage space presented a problem for Vanessa, as it poses for most middle-class Chinese, who live in cramped homes by Western standards.

Maureen was confused. "Why foreign brands?" she inquired. She did not understand why Vanessa spent on brands that did not bring prestige.

Maureen had read work by Tom Doctoroff, the author of *What Chinese Want: Culture, Communism, and China's Modern Consumer,* on Chinese consumer habits. Doctoroff, who is the Asia-Pacific chief executive officer (CEO) for advertising giant JWT, argues Chinese consumers tend to pay premiums only on items they use outside the home to project status but economize on items that remain inside the home, such as home decoration.

Vanessa responded, "I just don't trust dairy products made in China, domestic Chinese or foreign brands. The supply chain is a mess. I will spend more if I trust the brand and quality." Fears over another melamine scandal, or a botulism scandal, which struck New Zealand dairy company Fonterra in 2013, linger for years, and parents do not want to take any risks.

Her answer mirrored respondents on social media China Market Research Group (CMR) tracked and explained why foreign brands with cheap dairy products lost market share. For instance, in a project CMR did for a hedge fund analyzing baby formula, we found mothers correlated high price with safer products.

Many mothers responded they did not trust Nestlé baby formula, for instance. Nestlé located its dairy farmland in northeast China, a region known as China's rust belt. From Nestlé's perspective, establishing operations there introduced international farming and quality standards and helped local farmers and the local community. Nestlé instituted a cheaper price position than other international players.

But Nestlé's strategy backfired. Chinese mothers feared that unsafe chemicals from decades of industrial runoff contaminated the soil, poisoning the grass, the cows, and finally the baby formula.

Users commented that Nestlé's price level, often 50 percent cheaper or less than competitor products, such as domestic player Biostime, slumped so low that they worried about quality control. Nestlé's problems in infant formula show the dangers of competing on price in China as a foreign brand—consumers perceive that foreign brands from Western developed markets, such as Switzerland, should be more expensive than local ones, or ones from developing regions, such as Thailand or eastern Europe.

Once explained, Vanessa's willingness to pay more for infant formula, despite her relatively low income, made sense to Maureen—she had heard of the melamine scandal in 2008, when hundreds of infants developed kidney stones and five died, and knew safety issues continued to plague the dairy sector, despite continual nationwide campaigns to crack down on shady farming practices. But she did not get why diapers remained such a concern and asked Vanessa why she purchased Huggies rather than cheaper domestic brands, such as Anerle. Some diapers even had Hong Kong labeling.

"I worry about the quality of diapers made in China," Vanessa said. "Anything that touches my baby's private parts and skin has to be the best." She explained she bought domestic sanitary napkins for herself to save costs but "spares no expense" for her baby. She requests that friends traveling to Hong Kong buy diapers to bring back because they are "better quality."

When buying for children, especially during toddler years, mothers spend above levels they would otherwise spend for themselves—for safety—and they view those years as crucial for development. The one-child policy and competition with other children for too few good spaces in schools plays into the mentality and will continue even as the one-child policy gets relaxed because many are used to this mode of thinking and because high costs limit parents from having more than one child.

The state media has singled out many foreign brands, such as Johnson & Johnson's baby shampoos made in country, for selling products with inferior ingredients. Asking friends traveling overseas to stock up on infant formula, diapers, and cosmetics to bring back is common.

Consumers perceive foreign-brand products made in China versus overseas differently with a hierarchy true across all product categories. Traditionally foreign brands made outside of China gain the most trust and prestige, followed by foreign brands made in China, national domestic brands, and then regional ones. This hierarchy is becoming upended, however, as national domestic brands, such as Biostime in baby formula, start to source from overseas and position themselves over foreign brands made in China. These premium domestic brands are gaining fast favor and trust with consumers.

Fears of the made-in-China label are so acute that Vanessa bought Japanese shampoo brand Pigeon for her baby, despite holding negative feelings toward the country for the atrocities it committed during World War II, because she trusted Japanese quality control. She stayed clear of Japanese food, including sushi, because she worried it may be irradiated by Fukushima, but felt baby shampoo was safe because factories were based away from Fukushima and it was not ingested.

As Maureen saw Vanessa's spending habits, clearly Doctoroff's argument that Chinese won't spend money on the inside of the home is no longer true. Consumers evolve, no longer spending just to display social status. Alarm about food and product safety, as well as self-expression and individualism, are trumping ambition as the main drivers for spending.

Despite being six months pregnant, Vanessa refused to sacrifice on style. She wore shoes with inch-thick heels that cost $10. She wore a stylish red shirt, albeit from a no-name brand she paid 40 yuan (about $7) for. On top she wore a dark blue antiradiation bib Chinese pregnant women wear to block harmful radiation from computers, TV screens, and mobile phones.

Vanessa sacrificed makeup because she feared the impact of chemicals on her baby, but a quick look in her bathroom showed she spent a lot on face moisturizers and eye creams. L'Oréal bottles were strewn around the sink. She bought some herself; others were gifts from friends.

She kept a running shopping list, including nail polish and mascara to give her girlfriends and even their husbands, whenever they visited Hong Kong. "I ask friends to buy products at Sa Sa in Hong Kong because prices there are 20 to 30 percent cheaper than in Chengdu. There is also better variety."

Her desire to buy cosmetics overseas explains the *daigou* craze, where people buy products via third parties who make frequent trips over the border to Hong Kong. There is a thriving daigou business, with people setting up shop on Taobao and WeChat. Even with commissions, prices are still cheaper than legal outlets because of tariffs.

For clothing purchases, Vanessa's husband, Xiao Wen, stayed price sensitive. Stylish but no-name clothing brands took up his side of the closet. He did have a $600 jacket from Jeep, the licensed clothing brand from the automobile company that has caught on with well-heeled Chinese looking to show a rugged, outdoorsy image. He also had Nike shoes in his closet, which cost $250, because he wanted "the best athletic shoes." But no-name or cheap-branded clothing filled up most of the closet.

He had cases of domestic Snow Beer made by China Resources stacked up in the corner of the combination dining room and living room most Chinese apartments have. Sometimes he even bought regional beers—to save money for the baby, he did not think it necessary to buy expensive beer, such as Budweiser or even domestic Chinese brand Tsingtao.

Later we observed Vanessa washing clothes and cooking lunch. Storage space and packaging played critical roles in product selection.

She had poured 8 cups of powdered laundry detergent into a resealable old infant formula tin. When we asked why, she said most powdered detergents came in "horrible" and "inconvenient" plastic bags that were a "nightmare" to seal and store. Her favorite brand, a foreign player, sold products only in plastic bags and nonreusable cardboard boxes, so she took an old baby formula tin from a friend.

Until that point most detergent brands assumed Chinese shoppers were so price sensitive that they would shave costs by offering the simplest, cheapest packaging format—hence flimsy bags crowding shelves. But based on this insight, Maureen's company rolled out resealable plastic tubs for it powdered detergent. Within weeks, it emerged as one of its best-selling products.

The success of the better-quality packaging did not surprise me. Lack of quality packaging is an issue that comes up regularly in consumer feedback. One time we did a project on the bottled water sector, where we found the sturdiness of packaging was critical during the consumer buying process.

To be environmentally friendly, for instance, Nestlé's Pure Life water brand used plastic bottles with thinner plastic and shallower bottle caps. These ecofriendly bottles were popular in Europe, but consumer response in China diverged from the European continent. Consumers told us they felt Nestlé was "trying to cut costs by having flimsier packaging," and were concerned about the quality of the water. If the packaging felt so cheap, many respondents told us, they were worried Nestlé went cheap too during processing.

Consumers reported liking the harder plastic in bottles from domestic brands, such as Nongfu Spring. As one 31-year-old woman from Hangzhou told me, "I prefer the more solid feeling packaging from Nongfu than Nestlé. It just feels safer." This was even after Nongfu had faced quality control scandals but Nestlé has not.

Nestlé's problems also indicate a slight paradox—consumers worry about pollution but distrust ecofriendly and green initiatives. Most green initiatives might help the environment overall, consumers tell us, but pose risks to their personal well-being in the short term because the products might not be safe or are overpriced.

Vanessa began making lunch. She stir-fried chicken and drizzled on spices liberally. The scent made me hungry. We saw storage presented a problem for Vanessa. Her refrigerator squatted short and narrow—most refrigerators in China are about half to two-thirds the typical size of fridges in American kitchens. The few cupboards she had were so shallow that she bought compact and easily stackable products. Space limitations were a real eye-opener for Maureen, who was used to bigger American kitchens with ample pantry space. She realized her company would have to redo packaging across product lines.

As Maureen and I debriefed later that night over a bowl of spicy Sichuan fish, Vanessa and her husband's spending patterns brought to mind an hourglass shape—top and bottom heavy and narrow in the middle. For categories they prioritized as essential—L'Oréal face creams for Vanessa, Nike sneakers for Xiao Wen, and anything for their baby to come, they traded up and went for the top brands they knew of and could afford. For most other items—T-shirts, nail polish, and beer, they skipped midpriced products altogether. Even though Vanessa and Xiao Wen were middle-class consumers, they did not shop like they were, buying midpriced brands targeting middle-class consumers—they went premium or cheap.

⤞⤟

One warm spring day in Beijing, I met Wang Bo and his fiancée named Alice. Roughly the same age as Vanessa and Xiao Wen—in their mid to late 20s—they made about three times as much money. Alice had joined one of the Big Four accounting firms after graduating from Peking University, China's premier institution of higher learning, renowned for being the country's first modern national university, established in 1898.

Wang Bo graduated from Peking University as well and bounced around jobs at four companies over six years. Like many young Chinese, he constantly changed jobs to chase better pay packages and titles. When I met him, he had been working as an information technology (IT) consultant for a small Chinese firm for about two months, but he admitted he already planned to apply for other jobs.

But remaining long-term frustrations about the immediate future mounted. Wang Bo grumbled, "I'm never going to be able to buy a good home in the next three to five years. Prices are too high." His brow furrowed. "And what about the costs of raising a child?"

CMR's research suggests 28- to 35-year-old men who have not bought a home are frustrated and pessimistic. Ninety-five percent told us they were concerned about being able to buy livable homes. "I'm not sure if I'll ever be able to buy a home without help from my parents," Wang Bo confided. "Even with my salary continuing to increase 30 to 40 percent a year like it has been since I graduated, it's not enough to buy a decent home to raise a family in Beijing."

Wang Bo was relatively lucky in finding Alice. Many men cannot find spouses until they have bought a car and home, and this is even mentioned as a prerequisite in women's online dating profiles and matchmaking fairs, indicating a high focus on material security. One unmarried man in Shanghai told me his girlfriend refused to marry him until he bought a home.

Unlike Vanessa and Xiao Wen, who had taken out a mortgage with their own money for their modest Chengdu apartment, Wang Bo planned to buy a home with help from his parents. He planned to delay having a baby until he was financially more stable—he estimated that would be sometime in his mid to late 30s.

When in their early 20s, Wang Bo and Alice conformed to the same hourglass-shaped spending patterns as Vanessa and Xiao Wen in Chengdu. In those days, they thought they would get rich one day and bought products to show the status they aspired to. Alice had bought a Louis Vuitton (LV) bag right after she graduated from university, saving up several months' salary. Wang Bo had bought an Omega watch and a Zegna suit to wear to work.

However, as their future became more uncertain, purchasing drifted toward midrange brands. Alice started buying Coach and Tory Burch bags at half the cost of her LV bag. Instead of buying no-name clothing brands, she traded up for fast-fashion brands, such as UNIQLO and H&M. Wang Bo liked outdoor apparel from Jack Wolfskin because it made him feel fit even if he never expected to go hiking in the Himalayas or do extreme sports. More and more midlevel brands had entered the market in Beijing— such as fashion brands including Michael Kors, H&M, and MCM. Wang Bo and Alice gravitated away from the upper and lower ends of the spectrum toward newer entrants into the market that fit their tastes as well as their budgets.

For the past decade, Jim O'Neill, former chief economist of Goldman Sachs; Helen H. Wang, the author of *The Chinese Dream: The Rise of the World's Largest Middle Class and What It Means to You;* and other analysts have touted the emergence of an optimistic, aspirational Chinese middle class as the potential new growth driver for companies. That middle class is now the world's largest by head count—about 350 million people—who live in households making between $8,000 and $25,000 a year.

Able to buy discretionary items, such as clothes and cosmetics beyond basic needs, this group can dine out several times a week and afford to go on domestic trips annually and once every several years overseas. At the higher end of the range, consumers have bought one car, in the Toyota Corolla or Volkswagen Jetta range.

In first-tier cities, such as Shanghai, Beijing, and Guangzhou, middle-class consumers who bought homes between 2003 and 2008 got rich when housing prices soared. Investing in real estate then became the driver of new wealth creation for people now in their mid-30s to mid-40s. During the real estate boom, people got rich not from salaries but investing in real estate.

Until 2008, few restrictions on home buying existed. Banks doled out mortgages with down payments as low as 10 percent, sometimes less for those well connected. Encouraged by cheap credit and few regulatory barriers, savvy investors bought multiple homes. Many of my friends quit jobs at high-paying jobs to flip homes. One friend, a managing director at a bulge-bracket investment bank, quit his job, bought 10 homes for about $500,000 apiece, and sold them for $2 million each, netting $15 million in profit. Prices soared so quickly that speculators often bought homes sight unseen and flipped them without ever having entered the premises.

People who did not buy a home during that period missed what very well could be the greatest wealth creation opportunity in the history of the world. A stable political climate, booming economic growth, and an abundance of sudden millionaires encouraged a can-do spirit similar to the era after World War II in America.

Consumers' optimism led them to set sights high as they climbed up the social ladder. They didn't think of themselves as permanently middle class—for the most part they hadn't been born middle class and didn't see themselves as ending up middle class either. The hourglass consumption pattern emerged—they traded up in categories they valued, because they thought they were on their way to riches and wanted to show off their success so far, and skimped on categories they valued less. Anything in the middle they ignored.

To capture optimism, brands marketed products as aspiration plays often positioned higher than in home markets. This strategy worked well for many years. Take the Danish shoe brand Ecco. Known for being comfortable and relatively affordable in Europe, Ecco positioned itself as premium and comfortable in China, with the most popular shoes selling in the $400 to $800 range in China versus $100 to $200 in America. Luxury buyers told CMR they often chose between Gucci and Ecco. Another example is Samsonite. Often littering discount outlets, such as Marshall's or TJ Maxx in America, Samsonite reinvented itself for China as the premium luggage choice to aspire to, on par with German luggage maker RIMOWA. They opened stand-alone stores in exclusive shopping malls.

Yet, starting in early 2013, middle-class optimism in first-tier cities ebbed. Housing prices continued to go up, but salary increases did not keep pace, leading to desperation. Men felt they could no longer attain the dream of owning decent homes. Multinationals and state-owned enterprises alike cut back on expansion plans because of weaker economic numbers, limiting opportunities on the work front. Worries about pollution became more acute as Beijing and Shanghai experienced epic bad air days and air-quality apps proliferated so that people could quantify just how bad the air was for the first time.

Rising frustration in first-tier cities resulted in a dramatic shift starting in 2013 in how middle-class consumers began to think about their lives—and started to affect their spending priorities. Because middle-class consumers missed the real estate boom, they realized they might not all get super rich. They settled for brands, such as UNIQLO and Ochirly, targeted at the middle class and were more willing to express their own individuality by buying niche brands. If they could not be rich, they could at least be different.

Consumers reprioritized product categories they spent money on—cutting back on apparel and footwear purchases and spending more on experiences, such as travel, eating out, and movies. Spending money moved from emphasis on displaying status to focus on quality of life.

In second-tier cities, such as Chengdu, where Vanessa and Xiao Wen live, and smaller provincial cities where wage growth remains strong, aspiration brand positioning still works but no longer is as effective in major cities. Consumers in lower-tier cities remain optimistic as they experience gains from urbanization: Infrastructure spending and the relocation of companies to more affordable areas are creating wage growth.

Brands need to be ready to adjust strategies, because what worked three years ago definitely won't work three years from now. Consumer frustrations in first-tier cities might be replicated elsewhere in the country if wage growth does not keep up with housing prices.

⧫

Although analysts such as Jim O'Neill still tout the emergence of China's middle class, CMR research has found consumers on the lower end of the income spectrum in urban areas, making $350 to $600 a month, are far more optimistic than middle-class Chinese. About 875 million lower-income Chinese are just starting to have enough disposable income to catch the interest of brands. Executives need to understand the ambitions and drivers changing this consumer segment because they will drive profits in the coming decade.

As the economy shifts away from physical work, lower-income Chinese, especially women, are finding higher-paying jobs in the services sector. Salaries in this segment are rising 20 percent or more a year.

I met Little Yang in Shanghai in 2003. From a small village in the mountains of Sichuan in western China, she left her hometown at age 16 to toil in a Taiwanese-owned electronics components factory in Dongguan, Guangdong province. With $120 a month in wages, she sent half home; the other half she spent on clothes, shoes, cheap mobile phones, and time in Internet cafes instant messaging on QQ with friends. Her favorite shoes were a pair of knockoff Nikes, although she thought they might as well have been real, because "the quality was so good and there was a Nike factory nearby."

After a few months she quit and moved to Shanghai. Her older sister labored in a factory there, but Little Yang didn't want to join her. "I didn't want to work in a factory again—too boring!" When I met her, she was a foot masseuse in a parlor near my home. Although it was a legitimate operation, she had a don't ask, don't tell policy about her job with her family. "I didn't tell my family—they would think I did bad things," she said because her father was very traditional. Even her sister, whom she lived with, didn't ask her where she was working. By then she was making $180 a month at the massage parlor.

Over the next five years, I saw her for weekly foot massages. The price of her foot massages tripled over that period, and

Little Yang's salary went up at a commensurate rate. She still sent a portion of her wages home but was saving to buy an apartment in her hometown. Housing prices in her hometown had doubled between 2003 and 2007, she told me, so she was rushing to save as much as she could to buy a home before prices rose even more.

But no matter how much she sent home or saved for that apartment, Little Yang always had the newest, hottest mobile phone. In 2005 it was the slim Motorola RAZR flip phone. By 2008 it was a sleek iPhone 3G. Each phone cost two to three months of her salary. I always marveled at how much of their incomes Little Yang and other young people in China spent on their mobile phones. Indeed, CMR found in surveys we conducted in 2007 and 2008 that after a house and car, mobile phones were the most valued possession for consumers under the age of 26. By 2011 trips abroad, luxury accessories, and dining out with friends had overtaken phones in CMR's desirability polls— by that point smartphones had become commoditized, and many saw no significant difference between a cheaper Huawei or Xiaomi and a higher-end Samsung or HTC.

One day in 2008, around the time of the Beijing Olympics, Little Yang told me she was leaving the massage parlor. I asked her what she wanted to do next, and she said, "I don't know. Maybe get a job in an insurance company." She had only finished junior high (although this led to the other masseuses nicknaming her "the educated one"), but Little Yang thought she could find work as a secretary somewhere.

I didn't see her for about five years. Then one day she saw me at a Starbucks in a major shopping district in Shanghai. Instead of the cute little girl I had known before, she was a fashionable professional woman. Her hair, once straight and plain, was now styled and streaked blond. She wore a dress that stopped just above the knees and toted a Coach handbag. She waved and called me by my Chinese name: "Xiao Shan (or Little Mountain)!"

We started to talk about what she had been up to. She had married a man from Dongbei, had a two-year-old daughter, and was now indeed working in an insurance company—only in a sales position rather than as a secretary. She earned $1,280 a month—triple her husband's income working in construction. When they first married, they had made the same salary.

I asked if she had bought a house yet. She beamed and said, "I bought one in my hometown in Sichuan. We are all going to move there eventually. For now, my grandparents and parents are living there, watching over my daughter while my husband and I work here." The house was in her name, she told me. "I paid most of the down payment." Even though her husband had contributed as well, he agreed for the deed to be in her name to give her security to stop him from straying because she would keep the home in case of a divorce. Little Yang's experience mirrored research CMR has conducted—many women, especially blue-collar ones, are the ones buying homes or deeds remain in their names.

As the economy shifts away from heavy investment, women, especially in lower income brackets, emerge as the big winners, outearning men and changing family dynamics. Little Yang said, "Life is good and it is getting better. I am actually moving to Wuhan because I think the opportunities are better there. It will be cheaper for me to go home to visit my daughter." Her husband was willing to follow her.

⬙

Leta Hong Fincher, a sociologist currently finishing her dissertation at Tsinghua University, published in 2014 *Leftover Women: The Resurgence of Gender Inequality in China,* in which she argues Chinese women have largely been shut out of probably the biggest accumulation of wealth in human history as China's economy has more than tripled from $202.46 billion in 1980 to $6,988.47 in 2011 in today's dollars. She argues most homes are in the male's name because of traditional values in the older generations, where the husband's parents often help subsidize the costs of new homes.[1]

But flaws in Fincher's research make her conclusions suspect—namely, the size and consistency of her sample. She admitted in an interview for the website Shanghaiist that she had a 283-person sample size from across China that consisted primarily of college-educated individuals in their 20s or early 30s. She also conducted in Beijing and Shanghai personal, in-depth interviews that ran several hours long with 60 people, including men, but more women.

Fincher's sample size, methodology (online surveys), and selection of interview targets make her research questionable and not representative of the entire country. She might be able to draw a conclusion that college-educated women in their 20s and 30s in Beijing and Shanghai might have missed out on the real estate boom (I would argue against this based on more interviews CMR has conducted), but she certainly cannot draw conclusions for all Chinese women.

CMR's research has found the opposite of Fincher's—in thousands of interviews with women throughout the country at different economic and education levels, we found many homes were bought solely in the wife's name or at least under both partners. Female respondents said men did this to show security and love, as in the case of Little Yang.

Partially because of changing gender norms, but also owing to China's skewed male/female ratio, men have to go out of their way to court women and show that they will care for them. To show this, more and more deeds to homes are being put in the wife's name. Even among wealthier Chinese, homes are still very often in the wife's name, in many cases for tax purposes, to provide a bulwark in case the husband is arrested for corruption and to provide security for the women in case of divorce.

If anything, middle-class people now in their 20s, such as Wang Bo and Alice—not women specifically—have been shut out of the real estate boom, which is why we have seen increasing pessimism among consumers who have not yet bought apartments.

The housing boom if anything has empowered migrant Chinese women because they command higher salaries in big cities than most men can but buy apartments back in the countryside, where prices are cheaper. Traditional gender roles are going out the window as brains, rather than brute strength, translate into higher-paying jobs. That shift in gender working roles arguably helps explain why the gender imbalance is less pronounced in urban areas, around 110 to 112 males for every 100 females born, and much closer to the biologically standard rate of 103 to 108 for every 100 females.

As the economy shifts more toward services, women are the ones disproportionately getting the better, higher-paying jobs, illustrated by the average wage for a house cleaner in Shanghai, which runs between 4,000 and 6,000 renminbi (RMB) a month—between about $660 and $1,000. Wages are on the rise across the board for lower-end jobs—for men and women alike but women are seeing the fastest gains. Of China's 32 provinces and regions, 26 raised minimum wages by an average of 18 percent in 2014. Even wealthy cities, such as Shenzhen in Guangdong province, got a 13 percent hike. Although middle-class Chinese are becoming more pessimistic, lower-income Chinese have emerged as the most optimistic major consumer segment in the country.

In the white-collar sector, women are also seeing fast wage gains. As one human resource manager in a Fortune 500 firm told me, she actively recruited women over men, saying they were easier to train and did not job hop as frequently as men did. I thought of Wang Bo in Beijing, who seemed to change jobs every few months whereas Alice had stayed with one company since graduation. Women often outnumber men in Fortune 1,000 office jobs as much as three to one for this reason.

⤜⤐

Meet Fat Feng. She looks much older than the 29 years she claims. Her hands are coarse from manual work, and her skin is leathery from too many days outside in the sun. As her nickname suggests, she is a little more than plump (nicknames such as Fat or Fatty are often applied in China out of affection and are usually not considered insults). Fat Feng is from Rugao, a small (by Chinese standards) city of 1.45 million people in Jiangsu province on the east coast of China. She makes $250 a month as a street-side vendor selling cheap clothes. For her, though, the future is now. Her spending habits contrast greatly with how many economists think someone of a lower income bracket should and would spend.

As she gets wealthier, she does not buy more products geared toward her income level. Instead of buying more cheap buns and rice, for instance, to keep herself healthy, she actually skips meals so that she can dine out more often in middle-class restaurants. She visits Starbucks occasionally to buy a $5 grande latte and to buy toys, such as Legos, for her three-year-old daughter.

Many brand managers I speak with think poor people only buy products targeting poor people and fume about rising income inequality. But CMR's research shows, perhaps surprisingly, that lower-income Chinese are marked with optimism. Their salaries are soaring and food inflation has hovered around 2 percent in

2014, much lower than the 10 to 15 percent ranges between 2008 and 2011. Understanding how lower-income Chinese think and want to spend their disposable income will be crucial for brands in the coming decade.

As Abhijit Banerjee and Esther Duflo found in their book, *Poor Economics: A Radical Rethinking of the Way to Fight Global Poverty*, lower-income people do not just buy more cheaper items as they get wealthier but also often buy more expensive items. In their research, Banerjee and Duflo show that poor Indonesians did not eat more carbohydrate starches, such as rice or buns, as incomes rose. Instead, they bought more expensive packaged foods and often went hungry to afford them, which they would not have had to do if they had just continued to buy more of the cheap stuff.[2]

I found similar traits when researching lower-income consumers in China. When lower-income Chinese get money, they aspire to buy the same goods middle-class counterparts want, as Little Yang did with her mobile phones and Fat Feng did with Starbucks lattes. I have interviewed many very skinny women who admitted to skipping lunches to save for items and experiences they wanted to buy.

Mobile games and packaged food (small purchases offering "luxury in a cup," such as Starbucks lattes and Häagen-Dazs ice cream, or Perfetti Van Melle candies, including Mentos, or Wrigley's gum) emerged as popular expenditures. For them, affordable foreign food and beverage indulgences help them display worldliness much as a trip to KFC did in the 1990s for middle-class Chinese.

Brands and investors too often make the mistake of neglecting the 875 million people who live in the lower income ranges. One Boston-based equity investor scoffed at me when I suggested analyzing low-income consumers. "They're so poor," she said, "Knowing what they want isn't useful."

Data points indicate differently—ower-income Chinese make half of what middle-class consumers do but see salaries growing 20 percent a year, but middle-class consumers' salaries are growing at only 5 percent. There are also nearly two and a half times more of them at about 875 million. What they want to buy will be a major growth driver for many brands in the coming years. Ignoring them would be a similar mistake that many brands did by ignoring the emergence of China's middle class at the turn of the millennium.

RICHARD LIU, FOUNDER AND CEO OF JD.COM

Richard Liu is the founder of JD.com, one of China's largest e-commerce retailers. JD.com went public in May of 2014, raising $1.8 billion with a total market valuation of $26 billion, making Liu one of the world's richest people, with his personal fortune soaring to more than $6.1 billion. At the time of the offering, JD.com was the largest Chinese firm to go public in America only. A graduate of Renmin University and China Europe International Business School, Liu has also studied at Columbia University in New York. He is one of the most visionary business leaders in China. I interviewed him to find out about the rise of e-commerce in China and to hear his views on the evolving Chinese consumer.

Rein: JD has become one of the most trusted brands in China with high customer satisfaction, despite low overall consumer willingness to trust retailers. How did you build that trust and how do you ensure quality control of your supply chain?

Liu: In the Chinese market, concerns about product quality have always been at the forefront of consumers' minds. In recent years consumers have become more sophisticated and increasingly appreciate the value of a trusted source for goods. Early on JD focused on ensuring quality and authenticity, first through our direct B2C [business-to-consumer] platform where we source and hold merchandise, and more recently with very tight controls over our third-party market-place platform.

When we expanded into the marketplace business we wanted to ensure that we maintained our commitment to authenticity. We select suppliers and third-party sellers on the basis of brand, reliability, volume, and price. They must be able to meet our demands for timely supply of authentic products and also provide high-quality postsale customer service. We perform stringent background checks on each supplier and third-party seller and the products it provides before we enter into any agreement. We examine their business licenses and the qualification certificates for their products. We also conduct on-site visits to assess them.

Our third-party sellers are subject to penalties including being removed from our platform, if they violate the marketplace rules, for example by selling counterfeit products.

The result of this attention to authenticity is that the growth for JD's marketplace has been slower, but we feel that getting the quality control piece of it right ensures our long-term growth and sustainability.

Personally I take tremendous pride in providing a highly reliable outlet for quality products in a market that sometimes faces challenges on this front. While we always have competitive prices, JD understands that quality products and reliability will keep our users loyal.

Rein: Considering logistics challenges, what is the potential for e-commerce to expand throughout the country?

Liu: Early on JD made a major impact in the consumer space in China's biggest cities like Beijing, Shanghai, and Guangzhou, as well as about 30 major cities in other provinces.

The future of e-commerce in China is smaller cities. While coastal provinces such as Guangdong, Jiangsu, and Zhejiang lead our sales in terms of online retail order volume, less affluent inland provinces have shown faster growth. Ningxia, Qinghai, and Guizhou were the top three provinces in terms of online retail order growth in 2012, and JD has invested in a strategy to capitalize on this trend.

In 2014, we have placed a huge emphasis on accelerating penetration into lower-tier cities. In third- and fourth-tier cities we tailor products to customers based on market knowledge and big data resources, while also accelerating self-operated logistic network expansion, and enhancing promotion and branding activities.

We already offer same-day or next-day delivery through our self-operated last-mile delivery network in key markets across China. We believe that JD's self-owned logistic network has become our core competitive advantage that consumers have come to trust.

We have also invested heavily in building out our app and mobile platform to increase our reach in these smaller cities, where often people use their phones as primary Internet access points. Our partnership with Tencent will help boost our mobile efforts. We have what's called level 1 access to WeChat, meaning that the hundreds of millions of people who use WeChat can shop on JD.com without even leaving the app—they don't have to directly go to our site or download a separate app.

Rein: What does the trend toward urbanization (China is set to be 60 percent urban in the next few years) mean for JD and e-commerce?

Liu: The trend toward e-commerce is inevitable in China. JD makes shopping for authentic goods so easy and reliable that we have no doubt consumers will continue to move in this direction, regardless of whether they are in the cities or the countryside. Growth in cities obviously makes it much easier to scale our self-operated last-mile logistics network, but consumers in rural areas also highly value our guarantee of authenticity and massive selection of products that may not be otherwise available in their local market.

While income in the major cities is higher than in other parts of the country, inland provinces and smaller cities are growing quickly, and we expect consumers in these smaller cities will help to drive our growth. To prepare for this, we plan to further expand our reach into third- and fourth-tier cities by setting up and operating more of our own warehousing and logistics facilities and last-mile delivery services to customers in these cities.

Rein: What are the main challenges to the continued growth of e-commerce in China?

Liu: JD has always felt that logistics and authenticity were the two biggest challenges for e-commerce in China, which is why we prioritized them. Our self-operated nationwide logistics network solved the problem of unreliable third-party courier services.

In terms of payments, we offer cash on delivery for all direct purchases from JD, and many of our marketplace sellers also accept this type of payment. What's more, JD has acquired Chinabank Payment, one of the most advanced online-payment solution providers in China. We believe that providing a wide range of easy payment solutions will help to encourage e-commerce spending across the JD platform.

Despite the rapid growth of the online retail market, fulfilment remains a challenge for online retailers attempting to reach more consumers in more areas while maintaining or improving quality and efficiency. This is the main reason why JD remains so focused on investing in and building out our self-operated last-mile delivery network. We do not believe the franchising or subcontracting models for logistics, which tend to have limited value-added services, are able to provide the type of customized delivery services that JD can provide.

Rein: Why has groceries in China done so well while it has largely failed in America? Do consumers return a lot of products?

Liu: In the United States you see some online grocery services succeeding in major urban areas, but in China the opportunity is much greater. Consumers are used to getting products the same or next day through JD, which makes groceries much more practical. Further, JD has an online to off-line (O2O) business that cooperates with local supermarkets to provide delivery within 30 minutes. By leveraging our existing delivery network, we are able to significantly expand what consumers can get through us.

Design Products with Storage Limitations in Mind

OSIM, the Singapore-based massage chair maker, typically sold giant shell-like massage chairs to Chinese consumers. Despite being comfortable OSIM gained little traction in China because the chairs were too big to fit into Chinese-sized apartments.

In 2013 OSIM rolled out smaller space-efficient massage chairs. Square with sharp edges that maximized space utilization, these chairs flew off the showroom floor. The launch also coincided with skyrocketing spa rates for massages. For instance, massage rates at Congen Massage Healthcare Club, a popular chain of foot massage parlors, rose from 68 to 188 RMB over a five-year period. The combination of smaller sizes and rising prices created a compelling purchase.

Similarly, Steinway and Yamaha pianos have pushed upright pianos over grand pianos—these smaller pianos are more space efficient but also play into the demand for parents to enrich their children's mind.

Key Action Item: Limited space at home is a major determinant of what consumers choose to buy. Create products as OSIM did and packaging designed to maximize ease of storage, including being both compact and stackable. Launch several versions of packaging, such as refillable packages for liquid hand soap, which are popular because consumers will buy a more expensive pump-action soap dispenser from a brand but then buy cheaper bags to refill the dispenser.

Emphasize Modern Chinese Heritage

The herbal tea drink Jiaduobao, better known as JDB, outsells Coca-Cola and Pepsi in many provinces in China despite being twice as expensive at about a buck. How did they do it? By emphasizing a modern China rooted in heritage.

Chinese consumers of all ages believe in traditional Chinese medicine theories underpinning meals, including the division of all foods into those that have heating and cooling effects on the body. Oily foods, such as Chinese hot pot, fried chicken, and French fries are viewed as *heaty* and creating *fire* in the body, resulting in skin blemishes, such as pimples. JDB positions itself not only as tasting good but also as helping reduce fire using a recipe developed from its license from a 100-year-old Chinese pharmaceutical company. Lower-income Chinese will often treat themselves out to a meal at McDonald's but want to offset fried food with herbal tea for health purposes.

In its advertising, JDB uses good-looking Chinese men and women frolicking on beaches to make traditional Chinese heritage cool, exciting, and relevant for younger consumers.

Another illustration of this shift toward pride in traditional Chinese culture is exemplified by Ye Mingzi, known as Wendy Ye in English. Ye is the granddaughter of Marshal Ye Jianying and my wife's cousin. Famed for designing haute couture gowns and being a judge on TV talent competitions, she has begun designing pieces for Swarovski and more affordable products. Her goal is to push more for creativity and respect for Chinese traditions in today's art and fashion industries. She told me Chinese no longer want to just copy Westerners anymore but want to create for China specifically and have pride in their culture.

She has created a flower of life motif that is based on design in Beijing's Forbidden City. Ye told me, "Chinese should respect traditions yet modernize them."

Key Action Item: Consumers are often willing to buy and pay more for brands that are rooted in traditional Chinese culture as in JDB's case. There is rising nationalism and pride in Chineseness as a label, which explains the popularity of Ye's products. Being foreign is no longer enough for foreign brands to position their wares.

8

SEEING THE
WORLD

U ntil the 2014 military coup, Thailand had emerged as one
of the hottest destinations for Chinese tourists. Driven by
the comedy *Lost in Thailand* (the film, released in 2012, became
the first domestic Chinese movie to cross the $1 billion renminbi
(RMB) threshold, which is $160 million), Chinese tourists
flocked to the land of smiles.

The year before the movie's release, 1.7 million Chinese visited,
reaching 4.7 million in 2013. American tourists comparatively
declined from 694,000 to 611,000 between 2006 and 2010. In
2013, in a China Market Research Group (CMR) survey of 1,000
consumers in eight cities, Thailand was on the list of countries 87
percent of respondents said they expected to visit in the next
five years.

One sunny day in Khao Lak, a beachside town on the Andaman
Sea, I met one of Thailand's biggest hotel investors. As we sat
under swaying palm trees and the bright sun, drinking coconut

milk, the hotelier told me guests from mainland China and Russia accounted for 70 percent of occupancy in his prime luxury hotel in Phuket, up from 5 percent three years earlier. More than Europeans, these newcomers splurged on the most expensive suites and villas.

Facing spending cutbacks from his main French and German clientele, we strategized how to attract more mainland tourists to his existing properties when he suddenly remarked, "I'm not sure I want to cater more to mainlanders at my current properties."

His statement took me aback. Why would he not want to attract a fast-growing and high-spending group? We had just spent two hours discussing ways to attract more of this segment, so I became slightly perplexed.

I pressed the hotelier for his change of heart. He ordered a cold beer from the waiter and sighed. He said, "The problem with Chinese tourists is that their wants are so different from Europeans and Americans. Can I really cater to all of them?"

The Chinese, he said, want lively, louder environments where they can shop, play loud games at shaded pool areas, and eat in large groups, while European visitors prefer tranquil, back-to-nature kind of experiences. In other words, the wants were so different among cultures that he was worried about a clash of the civilizations.

"When Chinese, Indians, and Russians come [and] we cater to them by opening shopping centers or set up large group tables, we see a clash with what Europeans want. The Europeans leave for quieter hotels. We witnessed Europeans leaving Phuket and going to Khao Lak, Krabi, and other more peaceful areas."

These were all fair and good points, I thought to myself. For the next several days, the hotelier and I discussed the dilemma he faced. Can a hotel be both lively and peaceful? Can you cater to all groups without causing friction and without costs spiraling out of control, or should the hotelier launch or acquire a new brand targeting different segments?

The hotelier's challenges are not unique to hotels specifically because Chinese travel the world and their preferences often are at odds with consumers from other countries. For instance, Samsonite is considered a premium to luxury brand in China but midmarket in America. How can Samonsite manage the reaction from Chinese as the luggage they bought in glitzy malls in China is sold in discount chains in America? Another example is Coach, which is one of the hottest brands in China yet is becoming passé in America. Will Chinese women keep buying Coach if they see it in discount bins of outlet malls in America or on unfashionable middle-class Americans?

Some businesses might need to launch subbrands, spend money on renovation and advertising to appeal to more segments and to elevate a brand's position globally, or push marketing campaigns to segments for different times of the year.

My son, Tom, ran to me and clasped my hand. "Did you see that fish?" he asked, beaming. "It was so big!" He began reciting the different fish types he had learned in school.

We were at Atlantis, The Palm, in Dubai, which Chinese guidebooks tout as the world's first seven-star hotel. We peered through the several-story-high floor-to-ceiling glass windows of the Atlantis's private aquarium.

Impressive came to mind as I entered the main lobby and a mosaic of colors popped out from the walls. Dangling sculptures added to the majesty, and tiles forming underwater scenes lining the walls stunned with their detail and complexity.

I walked over to a friend, Sha Sha, who lounged in the lobby restaurant. I expected she would love the hotel. She liked the hotel, she said, but she looked disappointed. I asked her why the grim face. *How could anyone not like such grandeur?* I thought.

"There are too many Chinese here," she answered glumly. "I only like going places where there aren't any others, so I have something special to tell others when I go home," she continued. "I also like to share my travel photos on WeChat, but what's the point if everyone else has already been there?"

Replacing luxury items, the new status symbol is sharing experiences via WeChat. Before, people gained prestige by toting Gucci bags to show people around them physically, but now sharing experiences to friends via social media websites is the new way to gain prestige. Invariably when you turn on WeChat, you will see people posting shots of exotic locations they visit and delicacies they eat. Sha Sha expanded, "Obviously the hotel itself is gorgeous. I just wanted to go where no other Chinese had been."

I looked around. The lobby was full of Chinese. It was during the Chinese New Year (CNY), and it seemed all of China had relocated to the hotel. Traditionally CNY has been the time when people visit their hometowns, but now it is becoming popular to travel overseas with entire families. The Chinese Tourism Administration estimated 4.5 million Chinese traveled abroad during the Chinese New Year alone in 2014, an increase of 12.5 percent year on year.

The Atlantis had become so popular among mainlanders that the Chinese conglomerate the Fosun Group was planning to build two Atlantis-branded properties, one in Sanya on Hainan Island as well as one near Shanghai's Disneyland. Fosun announced in 2013 that it would invest 100 billion RMB in tourism-related initiatives, not including its stake in Club Med, the French hotel chain that popularized the all-inclusive package.

I was in Dubai traveling with a group of friends, some among China's wealthiest. None had been to the Middle East, so we took our children there to see the Sheikh Zayed Grand Mosque in Abu Dhabi, see Ferrari World, and explore the desert on safari with open-top Land Rovers.

The same group had been vacationing together annually for the past decade. Ten years ago, we visited Hangzhou, Zhouzhuang, and other standard mainland cities in tour guides. Then we moved farther afield within China, including Tibet and the Jiuzhaigou mountains in Sichuan.

After that, we traveled abroad to Hong Kong to shop for luxury products. Later, as buying luxury items became commonplace, shopping became less important. We traveled to Thailand and Bali to experience beach life before going as exotic and far away as possible became the point: Maui, Tasmania, and even South Africa became stops.

Now when deciding where to go, the top concerns are (1) making sure everyone can get a visa and (2) finding cool once-in-a-lifetime experiences that other Chinese have not gotten. As Sha Sha said, she "wants to travel to places where other Chinese have not been" and share her photos on WeChat.

Finding locations with few Chinese tourists is hard to find. For instance, the Maldives, an island nation in the Indian Ocean's Arabian Sea where rooms often cost $1,000 or more a night, is becoming one of the must-see countries for Chinese. According to the Maldives' Ministry of Tourism, Arts and Culture, Chinese tourists dominate travel to the island country. In the first seven months of 2013, 103,734 Chinese visited, up 66 percent from the same period in 2011. In 2013, tourists from the United Kingdom and Italy are the second and third most frequent visitors with 60,021 and 53,493 tourists, respectively. Mauritius, an island of Africa, is also popular, with the number of mainlanders visiting doubling from 20,000 to 40,000 between 2011 and 2013 according to the Mauritius Tourism Promotion Authority.

Chinese travel as exotically as possible and rarely return to the same locations. Unlike my American prep school classmates at St. Paul's, who would often summer in the Hamptons or Nantucket every year, my Chinese friends rarely visit the same place.

CMR research has found Chinese rarely visit the same property twice for vacation purposes and stay durations are shorter. Tourists often try five hotels in one week. They want to see as much of the world as possible because they were unable to travel abroad when younger because of money, passport, or visa restrictions.

The trend toward exotic destinations grows not just for the wealthy. Back in 2008, one of the heads of Disney's Imagineering department, which designs Disneyland theme parks, asked CMR to look into what type of destinations most interested Chinese consumers. He wanted to know whether they wanted to go to exotic locations or the tried-and-true ones, such as Paris, to design attractions for Disney's Shanghai park—we found even then consumers were most interested in little-traveled-to destinations. Sure, they all wanted to see Paris and Rome at some point, but they really dreamed of going to places off the beaten path, such as New Zealand, the Maldives, and Mauritius. They were hungry for new experiences—they did not want to copycat others.

No longer the domain of wealthy Chinese, scores of middle-class Chinese travel overseas. In 2013, 113 million traveled abroad, more than double the 50 million in 2010 and just a few thousand a year in the 1990s. By 2018, CMR estimates more than 200 million will travel abroad annually. In interviews with 2,000 consumers in 15 cities CMR conducted, the main reason Chinese want to go abroad is to "see the world" and "try something different." Chinese have become the new Japanese in tourists, disrupting entire industries, from hotels to dining to retail.

For example, retail sales growth over 2014 CNY week slowed to 13.3 percent versus 14.7 percent in 2013, but overseas travel went up 12.5 percent as consumers reprioritize their spending allocations and where they want to spend. Money spent overseas is soaring because shopping there forms memories and because prices are cheaper.

UnionPay International, a unit of China UnionPay, examined the habits of Chinese tourists. It found hotel spending increased at a 40 percent annual compound growth rate (ACGR) between 2001 and 2014. Dining was up 65 percent and entertainment spending more than 60 percent between 2013 and 2014.

Despite the opportunities, many countries put up too many roadblocks to secure visas. On my last trip to South Africa for instance, one of my friends could not accompany me because she could not secure a visa in time. The South African government required more paperwork for a visa than what she needed to buy a home, she said, so she gave up and vacationed in Bali instead.

Bureaucratic obstacles such as these are a mistake. Chinese are now both the world's most numerous tourists and the highest spenders overseas per capita. They spend on average $7,500 on trips to America and were the largest per capita spenders at the 2012 London Olympics.

Vacation destinations such as Bali, Indonesia, Jeju Island, South Korea, and Cambodia that have made securing visas on arrival or online in advance easy have seen tourist numbers swell. Yet countries such as the United Kingdom, America, and Italy are still losing out by not streamlining processes enough for the whole country.

⌾

I met Wang Yan one evening in 2014 in the ramshackle store from which she sells Nu Skin's personal care products. She now earned

$800 a month, almost double her earnings when she sold pirated DVDs in previous years. Originally from Guizhou, one of China's poorest provinces, the 34-year-old Wang had jet black hair cut short and wore stylish blue jeans and a tight-fitting black T-shirt.

As she sold face cream to an elderly woman, she said, "I want to see the world, see new cultures, and do things other Chinese have never done before." She whipped out her mobile phone and showed me photos of exotic locales she had visited.

She had been to Thailand, Cambodia, and France and now was saving up for her biggest trip yet. She was going to go either to Egypt or Mauritius; she hadn't yet made up her mind, but she would definitely go to Africa. Considering how little she earned, I was surprised at how widely she traveled.

Rising oil prices made transportation expensive. I asked how she traveled. "I always take the cheapest transportation available, whether red-eye flights or train. I even took a bus to Myanmar," she answered.

That made sense and explained why airlines schedule so many red-eye flights from China to Southeast Asia. Red-eyes save time and money—most workers get 5 to 10 vacation days a year in addition to 11 holidays but also save two nights' hotel fare by sleeping on the plane. Budget travelers prefer spending on sightseeing and buying products than on transportation.

One travel agent catering to Chinese to go to Southeast Asia told me Chinese only stay in cheap hotels to save money for shopping trips. As Wang Yan sold more face cream to another woman who looked to be about 50, I asked whether that was true.

Wang Yan agreed, in part. She said she always stayed in cheap hotels most nights—"I expect to be and out and about most days so [I] look for cheap hotels." She continued, "But every trip, either the first or the last night, I spend extra for a night in a luxury hotel to indulge." She said on a recent trip to Myanmar, she splurged on a $400-a-night room at the Shangri-La, equivalent to 50 percent of her monthly income.

Wang Yan likes to plot out arrangements by herself. Traditionally Chinese traveled in groups, often forced to because of visa policies that prevented them from traveling alone but also because they had little experience abroad and were scared. But that is changing fast. CMR research has found Chinese under the age of 35 prefer to book their own trips, going where they want at the pace they desire.

As I spoke with Wang Yan, spending habits for middle-class Chinese and Americans diverged. Instead of staying the whole trip in a three-star hotel, such as a Holiday Inn, as many Americans might, Chinese mixed staying in five-star and one-star hotels. Food was also another area where consumers went either really cheap or really expensive, spending in the shape of an hourglass. Wang Yan said, "I bring instant noodles to save money on food."

That made sense. Once I stayed at the Royal Begonia hotel in Sanya, part of Starwood's Luxury Collection, one of the most beautiful properties I have ever been to. When I walked by the housekeepers' cleaning carts, I always found them overflowing with discarded instant-noodle packages. The restaurants usually remained empty.

Many guests at five-star hotels, even the most expensive ones, are price sensitive people who save to indulge in luxury for one night during a vacation to experience true luxury. They cannot really afford food and beverages in a hotel, so they cart instant noodles with them. Often they dine once in the hotel restaurant to share the photos on WeChat with their friends but typically skimp on food spending.

As I said good-bye to Wang Yan, she told me to come back and visit in several months, and she would show me photos of her upcoming trip. She beamed as she dreamt about where she would visit next.

⋐⋙

Ajai Zechai sat across from me, the hot grill from a Korean barbecue restaurant separating us in the middle.

We both traveled to Seoul for a meeting of the Asia Council for St. Paul's School, where we both graduated from, but Zechai also scouted out potential new locations for a new hotel in the southern part of Korea.

Zechai does business development for General Hotel Management Limited (GHM), a stylish chain of hotels that include the Legian in Bali and the Chedi Dhapparu in the Maldives. Known for creating a distinctive lifestyle experience, with an emphasis on the land and local culture, the chain attracts only the most sophisticated and well-heeled tourists.

The hotel industry runs in Zechai's blood. His father, Adrian Zechai, was the founder of the Aman Resorts chain, one of the most exclusive resort chains in the world, and serves as nonexecutive chairman of GHM.

"Cheers," Ajai Zechai said, clinking my glass, and then we took a sip of Soju, a fiery Korean rice-based alcohol. Zechai divulged GHM's China strategy: "We plan to open dozens of properties in China because we see the demand as more Chinese vacation at our properties in China and globally." I asked whether Chinese like GHM's brand position of more intimate experiences.

"Developing a strategy for China is becoming one of our main priorities," Zechai responded, because GHM has seen a huge increase of Chinese guests over the past few years—it even had a Chinese buy one of its multimillion-dollar apartments in Europe.

"Chinese are becoming increasingly sophisticated and discerning in what they want," Zechai explained, as I plopped a juicy, perfectly marbled piece of beef in my mouth. *Nothing beats Korean barbecue*, I think to myself. Zechai continued, "It is not just about bigger is better anymore but distinct experiences, which is exactly what GHM offers."

GHM is well positioned to grab the shift toward individual and localized experiences. Standardized properties that look the same in New York as they do in Bali or Milan are becoming passé for many Chinese who want to experience local culture in more intimate settings.

Even traditional five-star hotels with great locations are starting to feel the pinch if they do not adjust. The JC Mandarin in Shanghai, with its huge lobby and grand crystal chandeliers dangling from the several-story-high ceilings, is a great example. One of the earliest and most popular five-star hotels in the country, the hotel shut down in 2013 as consumers shunned standard hotel chains to go to more distinctive, boutique properties.

The shift toward distinct hotel experiences that Zechai highlighted is similar to what John Galloway, the chief marketing officer of Hard Rock International, told me as well. Originally best known for its Hard Rock Cafe chain, rock and roll, and signature-branded apparel and accessories, Hard Rock has branched into hotels and casinos in recent years, becoming a hot destination for consumers looking for creative and music-inspired hotels.

Galloway told me the organization started seeing Chinese guests in its Asia-Pacific properties in Bali, Pattaya, Thailand, and Macau swell in recent years. Often Chinese became loyal to the brand and visited multiple properties.

For the most part, Chinese are not yet loyal to hotel brands, but by creating a strong niche, Hard Rock has created loyalty among consumers looking for a music-inspired lifestyle. These loyal Chinese customers have bought into the whole Hard Rock lifestyle, much as Americans and Japanese do. They have started visiting different properties, eating at the cafes even when not staying at a Hard Rock hotel, and buying T-shirts and other accessories.

The company decided to make a big push into China by doing a strategic overhaul of its operations there. It closed a franchised cafe outlet in Beijing that had not lived up to global standards and was not as irreverent and hip as other outlets.

Looking to find the right reentrée into China, Hard Rock found it in collaboration with the Mission Hills Golf Resorts. They are launching two music-themed hotels in Mission Hills' golf resorts in Shenzhen and Haikou, Hainan Island. One of the most perceptive players in China, Mission Hills found the Hard Rock brand fits into the needs of the evolving consumer looking to express creativity and for something new.

Hard Rock is keeping close to its core brand DNA but is developing the hotel with the needs of Chinese consumers in mind from the very beginning, such as types of music, lighting, and toiletries. They are not bringing the same music Americans like, for instance, but are bringing a mix of playlists to educate consumers about Western music while including popular Chinese and Asian music.

In interviews with 1,000 Chinese across the country where CMR showed potential design mock-ups of the hotel, respondents were "excited" about Hard Rock's concept because it was "creative," "unique," and "different" from the standard Marriott and Holiday Inn–like offerings. Younger and wealthier consumers especially told my firm they wanted more unique hotel experiences like those Hard Rock offered.

As one 34-year-old man in Beijing told us, "I am tired of the same five-star hotels in China. They all look alike; it is hard to differentiate. The Hard Rock concept is quite appealing when I am looking to relax and try something different with friends and family."

The response from Chinese who had stayed at a Hard Rock hotel overseas was especially positive. The vast majority told us they would "definitely stay again" because they liked the concept and felt "creative" when staying there.

For companies in the tourism sector, understanding and staying ahead of consumer needs is critical. It might seem like basic advice, but surprisingly not all companies understand the consumer as well as Hard Rock, GHM, or larger chains, such as Shangri-La. The habits of Chinese are very different from those of western European and American consumers, and the wants are diverging by consumer segment. Their evolution creates great opportunities for niche brands, such as Hard Rock and GHM, but it means challenges for long dominant larger brands, such as Marriott and Sheraton, because there is so much competition in the traditional five-star area.

Chinese consumers will continue to disrupt the tourism sector and associated ones much as the Japanese did in the 1980s. Understanding and adjusting to the opportunities from their rise will be critical for tourism-related companies.

Fritz Demopoulos, Cofounder of Qunar.com

Fritz Demopoulos, a graduate of University of California, Los Angeles's Anderson School of Management, first moved to China in 1997 as an executive with the News Corporation Limited. Rupert Murdoch once noted he can make money only from entertainment and sports. Taking inspiration, Demopoulos started a sports website, Shawei, that he sold to Tom.com.

After selling Shawei, Demopoulos became the senior vice president of business development for NetEase before starting Qunar. Baidu acquired a majority stake in Qunar for $306 million in 2011.

Demopoulos now runs Queen Capital, a private equity firm focused on global opportunities within the digital space. He concentrates his efforts on consumer-facing mobile and Internet projects, including online travel, e-commerce, and entertainment. He is actively involved in the Asia Society and the Young Presidents' Organization (YPO). I first met Demopoulos in 2005. I asked him for his views on China's tourism sector and the changing wants and aspirations of Chinese tourists.

Rein: Where did the idea to start Qunar come from?

Demopoulos: I cofounded Qunar with two others—C. C. Zhuang, a technology genius from mainland China, and Douglas Khoo, an online marketing expert from Malaysia. The three of us also cofounded Shawei.com, a Beijing-based sports portal acquired by Hutchison Whampoa affiliate Tom.com.

A few years after Shawei, sitting at a Starbucks at the Airport Express station in Hong Kong, the three of us determined to set up another company. At that time, our inspiration came from Google. Toward the end of 2004, travel advertising was Google's largest revenue stream, and probably remains so today. We thought, Could we build a better mousetrap than Google? Could we create a better user and product experience?

Today I am not a representative of Qunar, needless to say, but from my vantage point, Qunar is one of the most exciting companies within the online travel space. For the first time, consumers are presented with a full array of choices to book travel services, and travel suppliers are offered an extremely efficient and professional distribution and sales channel to reach consumers.

The first few years of the company were quite strenuous. Although we had built an amazing product, we struggled to gain traction. Possibly, we were a bit too early to the market, which has its advantages and disadvantages. The key advantage for us back then was that we had the time to build an amazing product, recruit an outstanding engineering team, and create significant barriers to entry before anyone else figured out we were onto something big.

Rein: Why do you think so many Chinese are traveling abroad now? Do you see the biggest growth and opportunities in domestic or international tourism?

Demopoulos: Overall, the growth in Chinese outbound tourism is symbolic of the rise of the Chinese consumer. After a few decades of amazing economic growth, purchasing power amongst consumers has increased dramatically. Indeed, according to several analysts, travel expenditure tends to grow at a multiple of GDP [gross domestic product] growth. China is already one of the largest markets in the world for many product categories, such as mobile devices, automobiles, and beer. The same can be said for travel products and services.

Chinese consumers, who are not fundamentally different from consumers in many other markets, are keen to explore the world. In fact, international travel is a "high aspiration" product, just as it is to buy a BMW, Swarovski crystal, Chanel sunglasses, Dean & DeLuca coffee, or a high-end Apple iPad.

Whilst there is substantial growth in international travel, the domestic market still offers huge potential. Like any large country with a long history, there is more than enough to do and see domestically. And, the result of increased investment in domestic tourism infrastructure is quite appealing to domestic travelers, making it easier for them to enjoy tourist destinations and experiences in China.

Rein: What changes do you see in what Chinese are looking for when they travel abroad?

Demopoulos: In recent years Chinese travelers were more focused on shopping and less interested in purchasing services, such as high-end or unique accommodation, spa treatments, dining, etc. However, we have seen a shift in consumer behavior where Chinese travelers also purchase significantly more services in addition to shopping for luxury products.

A second interesting trend is the fragmentation of interests amongst Chinese travelers. Previously, most if not all travelers were keen to visit the most high-profile destinations like Paris, London, Venice, and others. However, as consumer tastes become more discriminating and travelers gain more experience, consumers are displaying a preference to visit more exotic destinations.

Going hand in hand with the aforementioned trends, travelers tend to be keen to travel independently, which means forgoing the typical tour package. Yes, first-time travelers and less affluent consumers may still prefer a tour package. However, seasoned travelers and those with greater purchasing power are more likely to travel independently.

Rein: What differences, if any, are there between Chinese tourists' wants and Americans and Europeans when they travel?

Demopoulos: Anecdotally, Americans seem to queue up at Starbucks everywhere in the world, Brits look for a pub, the French complain no one speaks French anymore, and the Chinese incessantly look for Louis Vuitton and Apple stores. Putting that aside, I think independent, experienced travelers generally have the same preferences. Chinese, Americans, and Europeans all enjoy unique experiences, good service, and something to write home about.

Having said all that, less experienced group travelers may have different preferences.

Chinese don't really like suntanning and lounging by the pool. They would rather, generally speaking, visit the top tourist sites and go shopping or gambling. For luxury resorts and cruise operators this can be a challenging proposition.

I think there is probably a thirst for trying new things. A confident people with a lot of money to spend tend to try new things, and I think this observation is reflective of Chinese consumers as they travel abroad.

Rein: Many say Chinese simply copycat what worked in the United States yet you built an innovative company. How did you achieve that? What are the challenges for innovation in China? What did you do from a management perspective to succeed?

Demopoulos: We see a lot of copycats globally. During the group-buying investment craze, clearly, thousands of clones appeared in China. But, we also saw thousands of clones appear in the United States and Europe as well. Interestingly, while cloning is prevalent in China, a majority of the clones are financial backed by foreign investors!

Whereas in the United States innovations are more product- and feature-oriented, in China we've observed more value chain and business model innovations. Needless to say, our spiritual role models were companies [that] disrupted their respective industries, such as Baidu, Bloomberg, Amazon, Qihoo, and Alibaba.

I don't think there are any limitations to innovation in China. When there are massive opportunities within a highly dynamic market environment, speed and strong execution skills are more important than having the idea first. We built our company around highly capable professionals with a *challenge culture*. In other words, we constantly encouraged our staffers to challenge everyone in the company, to improve their skills and capabilities, and to ultimately create best-in-class products.

Very Important Person (VIP) Programs: Asia Miles

One of the great opportunities to create loyalty with consumers is with VIP programs. The majority of Chinese

CMR interviews say they are excited about loyalty programs, but a similar ratio say that current ones underwhelm them. Far too many programs focus on giving discounts and do not offer a global network of benefits.

One multimillionaire who regularly shops in Beijing, Europe, and America told me, "There is one major luxury brand that frustrates me because my status is not shown when I travel globally. The card I have for Beijing is only for China, which is ridiculous because I am loyal to the brand. Well, the program is not useful anyway because I just get discounts."

Companies should look to the success of Asia Miles for creating loyalty with consumers. Originally the loyalty program for Cathay Pacific and Dragonair, Asia Miles has branched off, and members can earn points at more than 500 partners and redeem throughout the world in nine categories, including hotels, restaurants, and financial services.

Stephen Wong, the chief executive officer (CEO) of Asia Miles, told me about creating unique opportunities for his program. The Stanford and Michigan State–educated Wong puts such an emphasis on creating value for his members that he often jumps in directly to come up with redemption options for members that are out of the ordinary.

The results of Wong's efforts have become obvious—in 2011 the program was named the best frequent flyer program at the Business Traveller Asia-Pacific Awards ceremony.

The Starwood Preferred Guest loyalty program has also engendered loyalty within China by creating memorable Chinese-specific awards. Not only can members redeem points for rooms, but they also redeem for shows to see

Zhou Libo, a famous stand-up comedian, from Starwood's luxury suite at the Mercedes-Benz Arena.

Key Action Item: Brands should create special occasions and opportunities for VIP customers, as Asia Miles does, rather than focus on discounting. Programs also need to be global ones, not based on city or country, as too many are.

Create Brand Loyalty during the Same Trip

Unlike many Western tourists, who like to stay at one property for a week or more and go to the same one year after year, most Chinese like to hotel hop every one to two nights. They also are unlikely to visit the same property year after year—they want to visit new places.

More consumers, especially younger ones, do not want to travel in tour groups, but they are nervous about booking travel on their own in a country where they do not speak the language and have never been. They often are more loyal to a travel agent than to the hotel brand.

Key Action Item: Hotels should offer discounts for staying at several properties under the same brand during the same trip. There needs to be more collaboration within the same hotel chain on packages, and transportation, to encourage loyalty to a brand. Starwood in Hainan Island has encouraged this by offering promotions where tourists can pay for a package to stay at several properties on Hainan on one trip and where they get food coupons when they check out from one property that they can use at another one. By having different properties cooperate on coupons and on packages, Starwood gains loyalty from consumers.

9

FOOD SAFETY

FROM CHICKEN TO COFFEE

When I first moved to Tianjin, China's fourth-largest city, brimming with 10 million people, in the mid-1990s, one of my favorite things was trying local delicacies. I would ride my rusty fourth-hand Pigeon bike and stop at frequent street-side stalls, eating pork-filled buns and deep-fried tofu. My Chinese friends warned me to be careful where I ate, but I did not heed them enough.

One warm summer night, I took a gigantic bite of fatty barbeque lamb from a Xinjiang-style kebab place. As soon as I swallowed I realized I had made a mistake. A decaying, rotten taste exploded in my mouth. Sure enough, 15 minutes later I rushed home in a fit of pain. Within an hour I started running a 103-degree fever. I did not leave the house for the next week, although I probably should have made it to an emergency room. When I emerged, I had dropped three inches from my waistline and become smarter about where I ate.

As I showed in my previous book, *The End of Cheap China*, food safety is one of the major themes driving consumer spending in food and beverages. By the turn of the millennium, Chinese were less worried about just filling their bellies like in the 1970s to 1990s but were worried about bad-quality food. In the drive for profits, many unscrupulous businesspeople emerged. They would bottle untreated tap water, dye vegetables with harmful chemicals, or simply sell rotten meat.

A government crackdown on selling rotten meat resulted in 16,000 festering pigs infected by porcine circovirus decomposing in the Huangpu River, which supplies some of Shanghai's drinking water, in March 2013—unable to sell the meat or pay for proper disposal, farmers dumped the carcasses into the river.

Fears over food quality explain why Western fast food brands, such as KFC, did well—they served authentic Western dining experiences and delivered hygienic and standardized food.

Consumers trusted KFC to use better-quality ingredients and control the supply chain. Trust reached such a high level that when the company became embroiled in supply chain safety scandals in 2012, same-store sales plummeted—consumers felt betrayed. My firm tracked consumer response to the scandals for a hedge fund. One mother with a six-year-old son in Chengdu told us, "Before I brought my child to eat at KFC because I trusted it to be healthy. But I won't eat there anymore because it doesn't seem like they are really that trustworthy after all."

KFC has spent millions in menu innovation, discounting, and renovations of outlets, trying to regain trust. It would have been cheaper if it had spent the money and time on supply chain management in the first place. Even with the added effort it might never regain the trust with consumers it once enjoyed.

When investors wanted exposure to China's emerging middle class, Yum! Brands was the go-to stock. Yum had generated more than 40 percent of its revenue from China alone by the early 2000s, and investors felt more comfortable trusting their accounting practices over those of local competitors, such as Ajisen Ramen or Country Style Cooking.

But Western investors often miss why KFC gained such popularity. Many told me cheap prices were the primary reason. Its price point of 20 to 30 renminbi ($3 to $5) for a meal may seem cheap to Westerners, but in most cities the chain expanded into, it cost more than most local dining options.

Far from a low-end restaurant, consumers considered it an authentic international brand that was trustworthy and aspirational in positioning—*not* that it was affordable or low end. I remember when living in Tianjin in 1997, young college students took dates there; parents rewarded children with trips to KFC. Outlets had air-conditioning, clean toilets, and even free toilet paper when those were rarities.

KFC's struggles can only partially be attributed to food scandals where suppliers used sick chickens and hormones. The brand deteriorated compared to wider competition. No longer an aspiration destination in first- and second-tier cities; it became a cheap one. Upscale concepts, such as Haidilao, a hot pot chain that emphasizes fun and great service (waiters are highly trained and even sing and dance tableside and bring board games for customers waiting in line for tables), and higher-end Western dining options, such as Babela's Kitchen, an Italian chain, have grabbed away share. No company has built the scale yet to compete nationally, but combined they chip away at KFC's dominance.

The closest any Western food brand has come to reaching KFC's initial position is coffee chain Starbucks. China emerged as the coffee chain's second-largest market outside of America, and

Starbucks expects to have 1,000 outlets in China by 2015, up from 376 in 2011. Young couples go on dates there, as do groups of friends and businesspeople for meetings because of the service; localized drinks, such as green tea lattes; and relaxing atmosphere. As one 24-year-old man in Chengdu told me, "I take dates to Starbucks. The environment is nice and the products are slightly expensive but affordable." Unlike in America where most sales are takeout, most Chinese drink coffee in outlets. This creates higher real estate costs per sale but also loyalty.

Spending on food continues to grow as consumers look for safer, healthier, and different experiences. The opportunities for premium entrants into the food and beverage sector are enormous.

Beverages are also an area seeing major changes. Take wine for example. President Xi Jinping's crackdown on corruption has actually in many ways created opportunities for new wine brands and concepts to emerge. Looking to buy more affordable, less ostentatious brands not associated with corruption, a new wave of wine drinkers is emerging and looking to try wines from different regions.

It was one of those magical, picture-perfect days that you remember when you are old and reminiscing about days gone by. The sky was a deep blue, and clouds hung in the air like big white puffs of cotton candy.

I had just arrived in Cape Town with my family. I was there to deliver a speech at an investment conference and then take a vacation, but first I was going to meet William Wu. A few days earlier my friend, one of China's richest people, had heard I was going to South Africa and said I had to meet Wu. He'd told me that anyone who was anyone visiting South Africa from China visits him. Within minutes of landing in Cape Town, we were in a car Wu sent, on our way to a vineyard, about an hour from the center of the city, passing Cape Town's Table Mountain and stunning lush vegetation.

Wu was at the front door at the vineyard's restaurant to greet us. Dressed in a simple but tasteful black polo shirt and white slacks, he said, "Welcome to South Africa," shaking my hand and tousling my son's hair. Leading us inside, he poured red wine for my wife, Jessica, and me. "Like butter," Jessica said, savoring the taste. Wu beamed, much like a cook when you devour the cake he or she has baked all day.

Wu had just bought the nearby Veenwouden vineyard the year before in 2013 to find a way to relax from his other investments in mining and manufacturing. He was the chair of a Hong Kong–listed gold-mining firm, Taung Gold, and an investor in a wide assortment of manufacturing companies.

In the corner of the room, an elderly Italian-looking man played a piece of Chopin on a grand piano. My wife and son went to the window to look at the rolling mountains circling the vineyard and to listen.

Wu pointed to the pianist and said, "He came as a tourist from Italy several decades ago, and just never left South Africa." Wu himself had first moved to South Africa 30 years before, during the apartheid era, and also had never left, even though he had arrived with less than $20 to his name and all his worldly possessions in one canvas bag.

It was easy to see why they did not leave, I said, gesturing at the natural scenery outside and the wine on the table—it was a big upgrade from the grayish black skies I had left in Shanghai just a few days before. A server brought over a juicy inch-thick T-bone steak and golden, crispy fries.

As I took another sip of wine, I asked Wu more about how his wine business had started. He said he had started sharing his vineyard's wine to friends at dinner parties back at his home in

Shanghai and found to his surprise that it was a big hit with his Chinese friends. "My guests started asking good questions about the taste and the production process." A few years earlier they might have just been asking how much a bottle cost, or how famous or exclusive the brand was, he said, but now asked about the type of grape.

Wu sensed a business opportunity. The days when Chinese only bought Château Lafite for show-off value, only to mix it with Coca-Cola and down it like shots (an actual experience I had at a fancy Beijing dinner party in 2007), were coming to an end. It had been rare even as recently as the middle of the first decade of the 2000s to see anything other than French red wines served at meetings and parties. But lately, Californian, Australian, and even Chilean wines had started showing up on tables.

As the server refilled my glass, I asked Wu why he thought this shift was happening. Wasn't drinking expensive French red wine a marker of social status, much like toting a Chanel handbag? Many wineries in French wine-growing regions, such as Bordeaux, were being acquired by Chinese companies and entrepreneurs and turned into export machines for the Chinese market.

Wu said he found his Chinese dinner guests now wanted to learn about specific wines and were becoming connoisseurs to "appreciate the heritage" and lifestyle behind it. They wanted to know more about how wine was made and be able to speak intelligently about differences in taste by regions, labels, and years. Many dinner guests to his home in Shanghai ultimately visited his vineyard in South Africa. Later, when I visited Wu at his home in Shanghai, guests directed the discussion at one point to know more about the heritage of his vineyard and how the wines are made.

Wu turned his hobby into a new business venture. He started to invest heavily in expanding his operations and hiring the right talent. When he bought Veenwouden vineyard, it was capable of producing 100,000 bottles a year, but Wu is expanding with the goal to hit 80 to 100 million bottles a year, most of it destined for the Chinese market. His merlot was the only South African wine served at the 2006 Nobel Prize–granting ceremony.

At the last dinner I had with Wu, several of his guests asked to invest in China to become his distributors. He looked at me and said, "See, the opportunities for South African wines are huge in China."

Wu's opportunity indicated a major shift in how companies need to look at the food and beverage sector in China. In the mid-1990s when I first arrived in China, most Chinese were still just struggling to put food on the table. Brands that positioned themselves as affordable grew. By the first decade of the 2000s, Chinese had started to look for premium brands, such as French red wines or Godiva chocolate, much as they did in the luxury sector. But as I saw in Wu's case, Chinese were now shifting to try something different. Wine was different from the mainstream, but South African wine was even more unique.

Wine sales for individual consumption into China have been soaring. In 2013, Chinese became the largest consumers of red wine, buying 1.86 billion bottles. Some categories have dipped because of President Xi's anticorruption campaign, which has prevented government officials from using state funds to buy wine, and from bingeing on the job, but wines destined for personal consumption have soared as consumers look to try new things.

Consumption trends are changing as more discerning consumers trade up from the low end, making it difficult for domestic Chinese wine producers, such as Changyu Pioneer, Dynasty Fine Wines, and China Great Wall Wine. Sales of domestic wines dropped 4.9 percent in 2013 alone. Australian wine sales to China fell by 12 percent by volume in 2013, but sales by value actually increased 2 percent as consumers began buying pricier Australian wines.[1]

To get a wider perspective of shifts in the wine market, I met with John Watkins, the chief executive officer (CEO) of ASC Fine Wines, one of China's largest wine distributors. Watkins, the former chair of the American Chamber of Commerce in China, first came to China in 1982 to study the language.

He has square shoulders and a matching sharp jaw. Watkins outlined a fast-changing market: "French wine is still the most popular of imported wine to China. Between 2008 and 2012, consumption of French wine increased 4.6 times to reach 15.46 million 9-liter cases. However there are many opportunities for wines other than French labels."

What other regions were becoming popular, I asked. "Consumers are experimenting with greater variety, and this includes variety in grapes in regions. For example, between 2008 and 2012, consumption of Australian wine grew by 147.5 percent, while Spanish wine consumption increased 6.2 times."

Watkins's views mirrored China Market Research Group's (CMR) research. We found that French wine still dominated the market but that more consumers, especially wealthy Chinese and those younger than 35 years of age, are willing to try wine from different regions and price points.

Barriers to trying wines from other countries usually boiled down to lack of education. As one businessperson told me during a project CMR conducted for a wine brand in 2012, "I don't understand wine—I always just buy the most expensive French wine in the store to drink with my clients. It's safer that way." In other words, consumers often bought French wine because they did not know how to appreciate wine fully and were scared to buy the wrong wine and appear uncultured in front of friends and business partners, similar to the way consumers bought entire outfits off mannequins before.

ASC launched the Wine & Spirit Education Trust (WSET) wine education courses to provide informative short-term training programs. The program has helped consumers become more comfortable with their wine knowledge and confident enough to sample wine beyond the most famous and most expensive labels. Watkins said, "There is a move from buying a wine because of its famous label and more toward an understanding of and appreciation for the *terroir* and how the wine expresses this."

Watkins' opinions are similar to what Belen Sanchez, the cofounder of Sarment Limited, a provider of wine services, along with her husband, Bertrand Faure Beaulieu, told me over lunch at the Kee Club in Shanghai: "One of the key characteristics of Chinese consumers now is they like to try new wines." Sanchez gave the example that many of her clients are becoming interested in how a grape, such as a pinot noir, from one country tastes different from another.

In the wine sector, like with food, consumers are moving toward new experiences, learning, and authentic tastes. Formerly dominant brands will come under pressure as consumers look for niche brands.

⌘

Since the melamine dairy scandal in 2008, domestic Chinese food companies have taken the lead at selling premium food products. Understanding consumers equate higher prices with safer food, they have moved quicker than foreign counterparts to launch new brands and products at the premium end.

Domestic dairy players China Mengniu Dairy Company and Bright Food started selling yogurt with packets of honey included at a 30 to 50 percent premium to Western players, such as Danone. They create eastern European brand names or import product from countries such as Australia and New Zealand to give them more upmarket positioning. Bright for instance launched a brand in 2009 called Momchilovtsi Yogurt, which relies on Bulgarian imagery and folklore on its packaging and in advertising campaigns. In 2014, Bright also bought a 56 percent stake in Israeli dairy specialist Tnuva for nearly $1 billion from private equity firm Apax Partners to bring better technology into its supply chain and particularly to bring the company's cheese to the market.

Western food giants, such as Mondelez (formerly Kraft Foods) and Nestlé, have been slow to realize the shifts in consumer spending. They continue to offer more affordable products in flimsier packaging than what the markets want—the result is that consumers are starting to trust some domestic firms over multi-nationals in the food sector. Mondelez's weak performance in China left it reporting in February 2014 a weaker-than-expected quarter. Mondelez chair and CEO Irene Rosenfeld said in a statement that results "were below what we and our shareholders originally expected."[2] Similarly baby formula maker Biostime received higher "trust" marks than Nestlé in a survey we conducted in 2014 of nursing mothers.

Large multinationals are being squeezed at the high end by domestic Chinese firms going upmarket and by the entrée of foreign brands at the high end, as well at the lower end by Korean food players, such as Lotte and Orion. These food giants have fallen into nowhere land—they are no longer the most expensive trusted brand but are not the cheapest option either.

Fear of pollution is also having a major effect on food consumption habits. Desperate about the effects of pollution, people are eating healthier, hoping to counteract pollution-related damage.

Sales of all-natural superfoods, such as Manuka honey, blueberries, and kiwis, are soaring through the roof, which explains why the New Zealand dollar has strengthened over the past few years.

Petrified of sickness, people are looking to eat as many antioxidants and nutritious foods as possible. Most prefer natural food sources over medicines, such as Lipitor, to boost immune systems.

Best-selling superfoods tend to be higher-priced items (Manuka honey often sells for $250 for a small jar) so consumers, wary of fake or artificially sweetened domestic honey, prefer to buy imports from reputable sales channels. Sales of organic foods do well, too—consumers often do not believe products are actually organic because of lack of trust of farmers or because of contamination in soil but feel there is a better chance that producers have better control of the supply chain.

⌘

To learn more about the opportunities for agricultural trade, I spoke with Eric Trachtenberg, a former U.S. agricultural diplomat, so to speak, who spent 15 years in the U.S. Department of Agriculture's Foreign Agricultural Service and now runs the consulting firm McLarty Associates' agriculture division. I had been introduced to Trachtenberg by John Negroponte, the former U.S. director of national intelligence under George W. Bush and former U.S. ambassador to Iraq, who now serves as McLarty's vice chair.

Trachtenberg has the friendly demeanor of a diplomat—approachable with a smile on his face—and wears professional but not ostentatious suits that show he means to be taken seriously. I asked him where he thought the best opportunities were for countries and sectors to benefit from shifting food patterns. He said, "The rising interest in novel and luxury foods have boosted imports in the retail, and food processing sectors."

These trends have particularly benefited imports in the dairy sector but have also "created a positive halo effect for imported foods in general," he continued. Going forward, Trachtenberg sees great opportunities in "tree nuts and dried fruit (prunes, raisins), fresh fruit (cherries, apples), seafood, poultry meat." These are all superfoods that consumers flock to, to lead healthier lifestyles in the face of so much pollution and stress.

Trachtenberg is seeing similar trends to what ASC's Watkins and Sarment's Sanchez have found in wine—people are willing to pay for novel and different experiences. The opportunities are good for countries that can supply products that China cannot supply enough to itself or whose safety consumers will pay a premium for.

Opportunities for imported meat and dairy products from Australia and New Zealand abound. "Brazil is a formidable competitor in the poultry sector," Trachenberg pointed out to me, and other products can come from the European Union, Thailand, Canada, Chile, and South Africa.

There are risks, however, for Western food suppliers. Political tension can cause consumers and importers to look for products from different regions, as has been the case with Norwegian salmon and Filipino fruits after government disputes. Within China, there is a growing trend against genetically modified food, which has become par for the course during production in many Western nations.

One senior Chinese official told me, "The genetically modified food sold by Americans to China is another form of colonialism. We cannot become too dependent on it and it is unhealthy for Chinese to eat this kind of food." This official was worried for two main reasons: (1) American companies sell unhealthy versions of food to China that make the population fat and sick that they do not sell in America, and (2) China's food supply will become too dependent on America, a security risk that would allow America to threaten to cut off food supply during political or military tension.

Fear of being overly dependent on American food stocks is driving decision making at the highest political echelons. "While Beijing seems to be moving away from a grains self-sufficiency policy, its investment catalogue has not been liberalized for many agricultural products," Trachtenberg said, citing increased restrictions in China's most recent catalogue on investments in oilseed crushing and continued prohibition of foreign investment in agricultural biotechnology. Prohibitions and regulations are hurting trade. Trachtenberg said, "China needs to accept that food security is not equal to self-sufficiency."

The question is whether friction between China and the rest of the world can be diminished the point where the government feels comfortable relying more on other nations for its food supply.

President Xi's anticorruption campaign with its emphasis on frugality has made waves in the food service sector. Restaurants catering to government banquets have seen sales plummet with the introduction of per diem limits and restrictions on dining or staying in five-star hotels. Facing slowing sales, 56 domestic five-star hotels in January 2014 requested to have star ratings lowered so that government officials would be allowed to eat and stay there again.

Some premium Chinese restaurant chains, such as South Beauty and the New York–listed peking duck chain Quanjude, have begun to focus on catering businesses for corporate offices. Instead of dining in restaurants, where angry citizens can easily photograph cars and share them on social media websites, state-owned companies are building nicer on-site cafeterias and investing in fancy executive-level dining rooms.

Chinese spirits makers Maotai and Wuliangye and foreign cognac players, such as Rémy Martin, have also suffered from corruption, KTV, and prostitution crackdowns. In CMR interviews with government officials, many actually said they were relieved there is less drinking at events. Officials were often expected to go glass for glass and shot for shot with people ranking higher than they until one ended up under the table, creating a toxic binge-drinking culture like that of college frat parties in the United States and even causing a number of alcohol-related deaths.

Restaurant chains have had to redesign seating arrangements away from private banquet rooms and large circular tables government officials favored to more public seating with mostly four- to six-seat tables. Interviews CMR conducted with restaurant managers around the country confirm that outlets that have made the seating switch are outperforming those that have not.

Although businesses based on catering official and state-owned enterprise banquets are dying, dining out remains a critical spending area for consumers. Popular casual dining chains, such as Da Dong, Crystal Jade, and Haidilao Hot Pot, still have hour-plus waits out the door despite per person spending often topping $50. Restaurants in hotels that cater to business-people and tourists, such as Shangri-La or the Waldorf Astoria, continue to see strong growth.

Over the long term, food and beverage spending will be one of the best sectors for growth—the combination of rising incomes, fears over supply chain safety, and the search for authentic tastes and experiences create opportunities for companies to introduce new concepts as well as build upon existing ones.

STEVE LIANG, FOUNDER OF FIELDS CHINA

I met Steve Liang, an engineer by training, for the first time in 2013 for dinner along with Harry Hui and William Chen, the comanaging partners of the Shanghai-based private equity firm ClearVue Capital who invested in Fields. TZG Partners, run by Ben Tsen, also was an early investor in Fields.

Originally from Kansas, Liang is the founder of Fields China, a high-end e-commerce grocery company that competes in the higher-priced food segment. I interviewed Liang about what food safety in China means for companies as well as emerging sales channels, such as e-commerce, which are threatening the dominance of brick-and-mortar stores.

Rein: What gave you the idea to utilize e-commerce when you started Fields in 2009?

Liang: Food safety was and is still a concern in China and throughout the world.

A bigger issue is that people in urban areas of China have limited access to quality, fresh organic products. There was a lack of trust and loyalty between stores and customers, which created an opportunity for Fields. Many companies (both local and MNC [multinational companies]) in the food industry in China need to improve their business practices, as their vision is often too shortsighted and they have much room to improve their ethical behavior.

E-commerce was the quickest and most intuitive way for me to get into the retail, grocery business. Consensus belief at the time was home delivery of online groceries in a large scale was difficult and economically impossible to achieve. It would be a logistics and customer service nightmare. That sounded like an opportunity because no one understood how to solve the logistics problem and it's important to be contrarian. Second, customer service and retail in China was in its infancy and service in China still has areas of improvement. With all of these barriers and difficulties and pessimism, I thought, *Wow, what an interesting opportunity and problem.*

Rein: What are some of the challenges for e-commerce in China?

Liang: China and the United States are different. Parking problems, traffic, and density here in China are much higher than in the United States. It feels like every Chinese city is denser and has more traffic jams than New York. Shanghai has a population of over 20 million. That's more than the entire population of greater New York. This makes fresh e-commerce much more potentially viable. And current retail and customer service is fundamentally weak, giving Fields this window of opportunity.

My belief is that for people to be healthy and happy, it's important to eat a diet mainly focused on local, seasonal, fresh products, not focusing so much on processed goods and imported pantry and canned items. This is where Fields differs from many e-commerce companies. We started from day one focused on having fresh products.

Another perspective: I didn't believe that China had no good farmers and artisan makers of food products. Food news from China tends to be overly negative. Much of it is deserved, but then it's important to find the great local farmers and artisans that grow and produce superior products and share their stories to our customers. China has such a long and rich history of food. It's just a matter of finding and rediscovering the tastes, the flavor, and people who are working hard to restore China's illustrious food history.

We need to change our view of agriculture. I heard that the average age of farmers is over 50. There needs to be a change on how we view farming and food. I hope farmers are the twenty-first-century rock stars.

Rein: Purdue is starting to control the whole supply chain with their chickens. Walmart has run into issues with control problems with the brands they sell with donkey meat and mislabeling of organic pork. How do you build trust with consumers? What do you do to ensure quality control of the supply chain and reinforce that trust with consumers?

Liang: Trust with consumers is through transparency, communications, and constantly improving internally. I really believe we should only sell products that we are proud to serve our own families. This resonates with consumers and builds trusts. And, I really believe in fresh fruits and vegetables. To be healthy and age gracefully, we need to eat more of our vegetables, especially ones that are grown locally. As we eat more fresh products, we start to respect our land and farmers more. I think this respect of Mother Nature has been lost in China.

Trust is being real and working on doing the right things. We want to build Fields into a company that every day does the right things. It starts with taking care of our employees and selling great, fresh, delicious products.

We spend a lot of time in operations, quality control, and everything that makes customer experience special. It's important as a business to focus every day on the fundamentals. We do most everything in-house all the way to our logistics. This allows us to improve quality and really train and get our employees to take care of our customers and themselves. We want our employees at Fields to really understand the importance of our customers. We need to take care of our customers and our employees the way we take care of our loved ones. People know if our service is genuine or not. I want the customer experience to be genuine every time, every day.

Rein: Which is the fastest-growing segment of your business? Chinese or foreigners?

Liang: Chinese market is the fastest-growing market for us. We are in China and Chinese consumers are becoming more and more savvy and they are naturally demanding for better products, better prices, and better services. We want to socially change China. Eating clean, healthy food should be available to the general public and not only be available to privileged. I find Elon Musk and Tesla interesting, inspiring, and a company that I can learn much from.

They make a great, high-quality car and they don't overcharge. They innovate, they constantly improve, they are accountable, and they work on making the customer service unique. Their car is not inexpensive, but they work on passing cost savings to the consumer and the car has low maintenance cost. That's what we should be doing, creating value and great products. It's refreshing to see companies wanting to help the consumer first. More corporations should be like [that].

Rein: Many argue Chinese are price sensitive and will not spend a lot. Do you agree? What type of products are selling well for you to Chinese and why? Do Chinese see a difference between imported products, foreign brands made in China, and domestic Chinese brands? What are the trends?

Liang: The Chinese, like everyone, wants fair pricing and value. The money they spend on a product needs to be worth the value. We have many products that sell well and for it to sell well there has to be value. Our local strawberries sell well as do our local blueberries. As do our selection of meats, vegetables, and seafood. Currently, for processed products and pantry items, imported products tend to be better. But I think there will be a change over the next five years. There is a community of local, artisan producers that are beginning to create high-end gourmet products. Our job is to promote individuals and companies and farmers that create awesome products and being sold at fair prices. We are finding more and more of these types of entrepreneurs. It's exciting because they are realizing simplicity is best and creating a value through passion and idealism. As an entrepreneur, I want to create a healthy ecosystem and help develop a community of people that are creating greater social change.

Offer Authentic Dining Experiences

When upscale Chicago steak house chain Morton's launched in China in Shanghai IFC Mall in 2010, it did little to localize its menus or store design. It kept its traditional beef-heavy menu as in America—although prices were doubled, at upward of $100—and deep mahogany wood and leather design. Ad campaigns mostly targeted expatriates and foreign businesspeople in China on business trips.

After opening, few people frequented the restaurant, by square footage the largest Morton's in the world. I often dined there and was the only customer in the restaurant. High prices kept traveling businesspeople away, and locals did not seem willing to dine on generous portions of thick cuts of steak. Six months later the situation changed and getting a table was difficult. The general manager told me the outlet has become the biggest revenue generator overall and per ticket over any other Morton's in the world. What changed?

Six months after opening, Morton's added lighter seafood items, such as salmon and scallops, to the menu to make consumers, especially women, willing to visit at least once. They also sold a smaller steak for lunch. Once Morton's coaxed consumers to enter, diners—even women—saw the thicker steaks, started ordering them, and loved them. Morton's succeeded not by making an Asian dish but launching Western dishes that kept to the brand's core DNA but were acceptable for local palates in both taste and size.

Key Action Item: Chinese are seeking authentic dining experiences. Brands should not be tempted into completely localizing for Chinese tastes, such as by adding teriyaki to everything, but restaurants need to make menus acceptable to taste buds and habits. For instance, brands should offer smaller portions for women and offer platter sharing. Because many of the diners are unfamiliar with certain types of cuisine, a large platter is ordered so that people can taste everything to see what they like. In group dining, one person has the veto vote, so brands need to make sure dishes appeal to different tastes.

Localization means creating relevancy, not reinventing the whole experience.

Perceptions of Foreign Brands

CMR's research suggests consumers tend to trust foreign brands from developed markets, such as America and Switzerland, to have better quality control of the supply chain. They believe brands from these countries should be more expensive than competing domestic brands.

Foreign brands from developed nations that try to compete on price fail because consumers will not trust them to be good if they are too cheap. In CMR research, respondents have perceptions of country of origin and pricing, with North America, western Europe, Japan, Australia, and New Zealand at the top as most developed and central and eastern Europe viewed as less safe and lower on the development scale. Having pricing schemes at odds with these perceptions usually fail.

For instance, hypermarket chain Walmart has tried to push its everyday-low-price brand positioning in China, which has not worked—consumers expect a big American firm to be positioned at the premium end. There are always cheaper options, such as wet markets, where sellers do not adhere to high levels of hygiene. Walmart's market share has dropped from 7.5 percent to 5.5 percent since 2010 as high-end grocery chains and e-commerce shops have taken share at both ends. Moreover, because Walmart lacks the scale in China (402 retail units, including Sam's Club) that it has in America (4,233), it does not have the same scale to force lower prices from vendors—in other words it often doesn't have the lowest price, creating a conflict between marketing and reality.

In some categories, such as condiments including mustard and ketchup, Chinese often want foreign brands and will pay a slight premium over a domestic brand but remain sensitive to price because Chinese don't consider them core categories for everyday consumption. They therefore will buy eastern European condiment brands, where they expect quality control and authenticity to be better than domestic brands, but are willing to accept lower prices.

Key Action Item: Brands need to price and brand their products based on consumer perceptions. A Swiss food brand can never compete on price with Chinese brands and still expect to build brand loyalty.

To offer more affordable price points, Western food conglomerates might need to launch a Chinese-branded product, acquire a domestic Chinese food firm, or launch brands from foreign countries, such as South Korea, Poland, or Thailand that are trusted but from where consumers accept lower price points.

10

THE SEARCH FOR THE NEXT CHINA

I killed many Vietnamese when I was in the Khmer Rouge, and I want to do it again!" the old man yelled at me, mimicking how he bayoneted people with sharp bamboo sticks. His breath stank as he leaned in toward me. He had rotting black teeth.

Age had not lessened the man's blood thirst: "The Cambodian government under President Hua Sen has sold our future to the Vietnamese. I cannot accept this. I will fight, and I hope soon."

It was a deathly hot day in Cambodia about 35 years after Vietnam invaded the country and a decade-long occupation ensued. As I interviewed people like the old man, there boiled an undercurrent of anger toward the Cambodian government, Vietnam, and foreign companies. Anger and pain seemed to hover everywhere.

I was poking around to see opportunities for the country to attract more Chinese tourism and light-manufacturing investment dollars. I was taken aback by the rage of the old man and others who told me they were willing to die and kill for their cause. The old man was the only one who freely admitted to me he killed scores of people during Cambodia's dark genocidal days under Pol Pot between 1975 and 1979, when 1.7 to 2.5 million people died from execution, disease, and starvation out of a population of 8 million, but not the only one who seemed willing to kill in the present. *How would that affect the country's development,* I thought with a shiver, *as I continued to interview people?*

China Market Research Group's (CMR) research suggested Chinese wanted to visit Cambodia to see Angkor Wat and other temples, such as the one where Angelina Jolie filmed her famous jungle scene in *Lara Croft: Tomb Raider.* The country held the mix of culture, art, and exoticism that appealed to Chinese tourists. The Cambodian government, to its credit, had proactively tried to attract more Chinese tourist dollars—even granting online visas for mainlanders.

The initiatives work. In 2013, 460,000 mainlanders visited Cambodia, up 38 percent from 333,900 a year before. Opportunities abound there to attract Chinese tourism—the hotel, shopping, and dining infrastructure remains inadequate currently, so investment opportunities there are good, especially with land and labor remaining so cheap.

The old man coughed, wiped phlegm oozing out of his mouth with his paw-like hand, and said, "I hate Vietnamese. Every last one of them." Trying to calm him down, I asked him about Chinese. His demeanor changed and his answer surprised me: "I like Chinese. They are bringing money and helping the country." Every day Cambodians had some of the most positive feelings toward China in my interviews compared with feelings of citizens from other southeast nations, who often complained about poor behavior by Chinese tourists, from tourists who carved their names in Egyptian temples to altercations with airline staff. For much of the world, Chinese have become the new ugly American, the moniker originally given American tourists traveling abroad who were loud, arrogant, and uncouth in the era after World War II.

Despite the opportunity for tourism, the threat of violence and labor unrest remains an issue that could upend Cambodia's economic growth.

Tension between the Kingdom of Cambodia and the Socialist Republic of Vietnam has historically been high in the classic big-country, vassal-state relationship. Many of the paintings in Angkor Wat temple show Cambodian heroes fighting off Vietnamese invaders. Bullet holes dot the temple today, a reminder of the country's more recent grim past. Animosity runs deep but, unless outright violence emerges, will not impact tourism. The tourism situation could be different from the manufacturing situation.

Drawn by low wages ($80 minimum wage in 2013 compared with $295 in Shenzhen in China) and cheap real estate, many apparel and footwear companies left China and flocked to Cambodia for manufacturing. H&M, Levi's, and Gap are just some of the apparel companies that have increased sourcing from Cambodia.

But labor protests in January 2014, when five workers died, and underlying labor turmoil threatens to upend growth as workers demand a doubling of the minimum wage to $160—without cheap labor, there is no reason for manufacturing companies to relocate to Cambodia. The political and labor risk is too high.

China has better infrastructure, a stable political system, and more efficient workers—it also moves in quickly at the mention of labor unrest to quell violence. Even with lower wages, the efficiency of Cambodian workers is a quarter of that of the Chinese. Cambodia often does not even have electricity outside of the main urban areas, let alone the ports, airports, and other infrastructure populating China. I visited many homes lacking electricity and where residents had to run off into the fields to defecate.

Many of my clients were anxious about Cambodia's labor situation and wanted to know how to adjust—stay in China and improve efficiency, automate as Catanese and Giraudi did with their mannequin factory in Shanghai, or continue to relocate operations across markets in Asia, such as Cambodia.

During my research, I was taken aback by the anger toward Vietnam as well as foreign manufacturers. In interview after interview with lower-income Cambodians, the majority said they hated Vietnam and were willing to use violence if necessary to get better rights in work areas. Sourcing from Cambodia makes economic sense, but risks abound—getting exposure to Cambodia would be smart, but the exposure needs to be liquid, without high up-front capital investment and with alternate plans put in place in case violence spirals out of control.

Unlike Japan, Cambodia's government has moved closer to China. In 2012, when China was chair of the Association of Southeast Asian Nations (ASEAN), it refused to address growing tension in the South China Sea. China has doled out $2 billion in foreign aid to the country, mostly through soft loans since 1992. In 2011, China's foreign direct investment (FDI) into Cambodia was $1.147 billion, nearly 10 times that from the United States according to the Cambodian Investment Board.[1]

Cambodia will continue to benefit from its closeness to China, because China likes to dole out benefits to nations that support it. Long-term capital investment is dangerous because the country could increase wages or have more armed combat with Vietnam or violent protesters.

⌖

Popular on bookshelves are books providing a guide to find the next China or economic miracles, such as Ruchir Sharma's *Breakout Nations: In Pursuit of the Next Economic Miracles.* But the reality is there is no other country with the size and stable political system of China—what is important is understanding how China's rise will affect its neighbors and how businesspeople can benefit.

I have traveled to many of China's neighbors to research the opportunities and challenges. Countries are approaching China in three main ways:

1. Nations such as Cambodia are moving closer to China's orbit, as a way to offset American power, and will benefit from increased Chinese trade, tourism, and investment.

2. Other nations, such as Singapore and Indonesia, are craftily building relations with China without damaging relations with America, benefitting economically from all sides.

3. Finally, some countries, such as the Philippines and Vietnam, eye China's rise warily, and are aligning with America and Japan at the expense of tourism and trade with China.

Companies and investors need to understand how China's changes affect other nations and the rising political risk and how China's government views potential threats. The big elephant in the room to understand is Japan, where ultranationalists are influencing Prime Minister Shinzo Abe and gaining considerable sway in political discourse. Incidents between Cambodia and Vietnam would likely be isolated to those nations, but tension between China and Japan has the potential to spread throughout the world.

⚜

One warm spring day around the turn of the millennium, I invited three of my Japanese graduate school classmates at Harvard to lunch at Grendel's Den, a popular restaurant near Harvard Square.

The conversation started as being about economic trade between China and Japan before quickly veering to the historical legacy of World War II. I brought up the idea that China wanted

Japan's government to acknowledge the past better, especially when it comes to the comfort women, when my classmate angrily interrupted me: "Uh, the comfort women again. They were happy to be comfort women. We paid them in a time when it was hard to make money. Get over it."

The statement of my classmate, who was sent by the Japan Self-Defense Forces (Japan's military) to Harvard, shocked me. I had read about people who held these ideas, but I did not expect them from a Harvard-educated person. I was too stunned to answer.

My other two classmates showed different reactions. One, who also worked for the Japanese government in the ministry of finance, displayed a benign smile and looked somewhat unhappy but remained quiet. He put his head down, not looking anyone in the eye. My other classmate, who worked in the private sector, looked visibly agitated and said calmly but strongly, "We cannot deny the past."

The conversation sort of ended there.

Most American businesspeople I meet underestimate the potential for serious tension between China and Japan. Many think that the anger in China is more of a propaganda tool the Chinese government wields at opportune times but that the anger is not deep-seated. Doug Young, a China-based journalist, argues China's leadership leverages anti-Japanese sentiment to divert attention from domestic issues.

But underestimating the palpable undercurrent of anger toward Japan among China's population that the government doesn't fan directly would be a mistake. If anything the government corrals the anger and directs to let Chinese let off steam but is not the main instigator.

As Japan's Prime Minister Abe pushes to change his nation's constitution to take a larger military role in Asia, waxes nostalgic for imperial Japan, and limits press freedom to appeal to ultra-nationalists—concern grows in China and South Korea about rising Japanese militancy. The echoes of World War II, when the Japanese Imperial Army systemically enslaved 200,000 to 400,000 women as sex slaves and when 35 million Chinese perished, are not easily forgotten.

Abe's maternal grandfather, Nobusuke Kishi, was held in Sugamo Prison as a Class A war criminal after World War II because he was Japan's minister of munitions from 1941 until Japan's surrender and had previously been accused of exploiting Chinese slave labor as one of the senior Japanese officials masterminding Manchukuo, the puppet regime installed in China. Many Chinese view Abe as if he were like a grandson of Adolf Hitler as president of Germany waxing nostalgic for the Nazi era.

If an incident happens over the Diaoyu Islands, a largely economically worthless island group consisting of five islets and three barren rocks that Japan and China both claim as their own, mass public opinion on either side could be inflamed and might not be something either government could control. Neither government wants to be seen as being weak in a time of confrontation, which could spiral out of control because America has reaffirmed its obligations to protect Japan in time of battle.

Investors need to understand the underlying reasons and the impact stemming from China-Japan unrest and their affect on brands in China. Whenever unrest occurs, investors need to be worried about two types of Japanese brands, such as Toyota, that (1) are closely affiliated with being Japanese and (2) are used in public and thus not something that can be put in a drawer or hidden in the house during times of turmoil. What that means is that the automobile sector and consumer electronics are especially risky whereas cosmetics, eyeglasses, and clothes are less so.

⊂⊚⊃

In September 2012 in Xian 51-year-old Li Jianli stepped out of his car to try to stop protesters, his fellow countrymen, from bashing it with bricks. Li was driving into downtown to help look for an apartment for his soon-to-be-married son when the protesters confronted him.

Video taken at the event shows Li pleading with the mob, saying he was also anti-Japanese and wanted to "protect the Diaoyu Islands." Suddenly, a stocky man named Cai Yang rushes on the video screen and strikes Li four times in the head with a U-shaped bike lock. Li crumbles to the ground like a rag doll while his wife cries out. The thug, after hitting Li, continues his reign of terror and bashes the Corolla.

Li can no longer walk or speak, beaten simply for driving a Japanese-branded car. The police later arrested Cai for his brutality.

Watched millions of times on online video websites, such as Youku, Chinese became scared about spending money on big-ticket overtly Japanese items. They did not want to be the next Li. In interviews with consumers, CMR found that Chinese stopped buying Japanese products more because of fears of becoming the next Li than to protest Japan. More than a dozen protesters were jailed for attacking and damaging Japanese-branded cars, reported the *China Daily*, showing the Li incident was not an isolated one.

When political tensions rise, Chinese will stop buying Japanese cars and potentially expensive, big-branded items, such as Canon or Olympus cameras, more because of fear about being attacked by other Chinese than for political protest purposes. The same thing will happen at Japanese dining establishments during periods of tension. People dining out are worried that fellow Chinese who are protesting Japan will pour hot soup onto them and stay away while tensions are serious. Incidents throughout the country of diners in Japanese restaurants being attacked by fellow Chinese have hit social media outlets.

The situation is different for products that are hidden, or consumed in the home, such as a Sony television or cosmetics.

Political tensions do not hurt cosmetics companies, such as Shiseido, for instance. Women buy the product, keep it at the home, and desire to look beautiful and younger. When you are outside, no one knows what brand of cosmetics you are wearing. Women are extremely brand loyal in cosmetics, and concerns about beauty trump political tensions. In general, it is hard to get a woman to switch from luxury cosmetics brands to cheaper ones. Once women buy luxury, they tend to stick with it; however, they are willing to try new luxury brands, which is why Estée Lauder remains well positioned for growth because it offers so many brands at the luxury level whereas L'Oréal, with relatively fewer luxury brands in China, might need to think about increasing the brands under its umbrella.

UNIQLO similarly is not overtly affiliated with being Japanese. During the protests I stood near UNIQLO to see if foot traffic dropped. It did not. One day I saw a family come to UNIQLO. There was the husband and wife, a child of about six, and the grandmother. The mother walked in front of the group and said, "I want to go to UNIQLO."

The husband grabbed her arm and asked, "Is UNIQLO a Japanese brand?"

The mother stopped for a second, while the child grabbed her legs and dangled for a bit in play, and said, "I do not know if it is Japanese or not."

The husband said, "I think it is but I am not sure."

The wife then said, "Who cares? The clothes are cheap and good quality. And we need to buy something for *Mao Mao* (the child)."

The husband shrugged his shoulders and said "Okay," and then they all walked in. I watched them and they ended up filling up a shopping bag.

Tension toward Japan is very real, and businesspeople should not overestimate the role the Chinese government currently plays in fanning anti-Japanese sentiment—it is largely part of the national psyche at this stage. Investors need to keep regular tabs on political tension. The main countries that benefit from Japanese tension are Korea and Germany. Hyundai and Kia benefit when tension is up, because more price-conscious car buyers go for Korean cars. Buyers consider Korean cars cute, easy, and cheap to maintain, and politically safe. Similarly, some buyers will trade up from a Toyota or Nissan and buy a BMW, Audi, or Mercedes.

⊂≫⊃

Indonesia—physically far enough from both China and America to minimize military risks over the South China Sea and blessed with natural resources China wants, such as coal, palm oil, and rubber—has done an excellent job at creating strong relations with both countries without alienating anyone.

One autumn day in 2013 I dined with former Indonesian president B. J. Habibie at the Jean-Georges French restaurant in Shanghai's famed Three on the Bund, one of the most well-appointed establishments at which I have eaten.

I was excited to meet Habibie—in interviews with Indonesians I conducted, he always had the highest satisfaction of former presidents in the era after Suharto. As one 26-year-old Indonesian man selling bird's nests told me, "Habibie tried to help Indonesia, was smart and educated in Germany but came home to help the country, and tried to stop corruption."

As a server brought over an exquisite foie gras appetizer, Habibie, who sat directly across from me, said with his eyes kindly twinkling, "Shaun has a baby face, just like I do." Slight in height, the 77-year-old Habibie looked much younger than his years—he had a warm, professorial, almost grandfatherly face that could easily pass for 60.

I took another bite of the foie gras. Heavenly. I felt like I was back in Paris at a Michelin-starred restaurant. I asked Habibie how he saw China-Indonesia relations playing out in the coming years.

"Indonesian relations with China are at its strongest point," Habibie responded immediately. He then continued to tell me about all the cultural and economic ties that brought China and Indonesia closer. He pointed out the large overseas Chinese community, about 4.7 percent of the total population.

Habibie was right—ties between Indonesia and China are strong right now, which will benefit both countries. If Indonesia can ensure continued religious openness, rid itself of the specter of rising protectionism, and ease stifling corruption, it is one of the most exciting nations for investors to look at because it beckons tourists and manufacturers alike, which is creating an emerging middle class.

Chinese are particularly interested in visiting Indonesian beaches in Bali. Like with Cambodia's temples, Bali is becoming a stop on Chinese tourists' must-see lists, with its beaches, volcanoes, and artistic side in Ubud. Easy-to-secure visas (mainlanders can get visas at the Bali airport in Denpasar), exotic local arts, and culture are drawing Chinese wanting to try something different.

In 2011, 470,000 Chinese visited Indonesia. The number soared to more than 900,000 by 2013. After Australians, Chinese are the biggest tourist group to Bali.

Nusa Dua, the famed five-star beach area, is undergoing massive construction to cater to the new influx of Chinese tourists. The Shangri-La and Marriott chains are both opening properties, and other hotels are adding rooms and entire new wings. There is actually so much capacity being built that room prices are dropping, but overall revenue is increasing because occupancy is high. One hotel manager of the Westin Nusa Dua, a five-star resort popular with Chinese, told me, "We doubled the number of our rooms in the last year in part to cater to more Chinese."

As the world's fourth most populous nation, with 247 million people, Indonesia is also one of the few countries that has a large enough labor pool to gain significant share from manufacturing. Salaries are half those of China, and the Indonesian currency, the rupiah, dropped 20 percent in value in 2013, making the country more attractive for investment. FDI rose 22.4 percent in 2013 year over year to $22.74 billion.

Furniture, apparel, and shoe companies such as UNIQLO and Ashley Furniture, are all relocating more sourcing and operations to Indonesia. Indonesia has links to overseas Chinese groups, such as the Lippo Group run by billionaire Mochtar Riady, whose linguistic and cultural similarities make it easier to conduct business with mainlanders. Foxconn, the maker of many of Apple's products, run by Taiwanese billionaire Terry Gou, has announced multibillionaire investments into the country.

Unlike other southeast nations it is large enough to play a key role for Chinese exports and as a market for Chinese brands, such as Xiaomi, to sell into. Tencent's WeChat in 2013 eclipsed Facebook as the most popular social media website in 2013. State-owned enterprises, such as the China Development Bank and China Railway Construction Corporation, are bidding for financing or building projects. Big and wealthy enough, Indonesia is not a market that China wants to ignore as it might be willing to do with smaller nations, such as Vietnam, to get political and military points across.

Indonesia's rising middle class is also fueling a similar demand for the brands that have sold well in China—Starbucks, Burger King, and Zara. As the nation attracts more factories, an emerging middle class will develop much as one did in China a little more than a decade ago.

Risks do abound, however, that could slow Indonesia's rise—specifically a vocal ultrareligious Muslim minority that could scare away foreign investment, as well as policies, such as banning nickel and other raw material exports, which is what caused nickel prices to soar 40 percent in the first quarter of 2014 and made natural resource investors more nervous. In 2013 for instance, protests forced the Miss World beauty pageant to move from Java, where there is a Muslim majority, to the more tolerant Bali Island with a Hindu majority.

If the government can stabilize the corruption and ensure ethnic and religious harmony, Indonesia could emerge as the next hot market for companies looking for scale. As I said good-bye to Habibie, he clasped my hand and welcomed me to visit him in Indonesia sometime and help continue to push for better Indonesia-China relations.

Aside from Japan, the countries that seem most willing to go against Chinese rise are Vietnam and the Philippines. In the spring of 2014, soldiers from those two nations partied together on the Spratly Islands, an area contested by them and China, to demonstrate that China was bullying the rest of the region.

Unknown to many Americans, the two Communist countries China and Vietnam fought a brief but bloody border war in 1979 where tens of thousands died. Relations have improved over the past decade but were still frosty when they became downright cold in 2014, when Chinese and Vietnamese fishing vessels skirmished in the South China Sea over the Spratly Islands.

The tussle on the ocean resulted in widespread violent protests on land in Vietnam, with protesters seemingly attacking any factory that had Chinese characters on signs. Protesters even attacked South Korean and Singaporean factories, thinking they were Chinese owned, putting a massive stall on tourism and investment there. In total, 200 factories were attacked, and reports allege dozens were killed before the Vietnamese government several days later finally stepped in to subdue protests.

The anger toward China by everyday Vietnamese is nothing new, yet until the protests most Chinese had referred to Vietnam in positive or neutral terms in CMR interviews.

When I visited Vietnam for a series of speeches in 2010 and 2012, I was surprised at the hatred many Vietnamese have toward Chinese, especially considering that 1.4 million Chinese tourists visited the country in 2012, the largest group to the nation. But the tourist dollars coming into the country did little to make Vietnamese like Chinese.

One tour guide who regularly took Chinese on tours told me, "China is the enemy, not America." I was surprised he harbored more hatred for China than America or France, which had long wars against Vietnam in the past century. But the tour guide told me that historically over the centuries China was "the enemy," with many street names named after Vietnamese heroes who fought against China's domination.

Although many Americans assume Vietnam and China are close because they both are Communist countries, reality is different, which clearly shows America's domino theory that led to invasion of Vietnam in the 1960s is wrong. The protests are going to make Chinese firms think twice about expanding operations there. Rumors abound that after the protests, the Chinese government told state-owned enterprises not to bid for projects in Vietnam.

Tourist numbers plummeted after the protests, with tour groups canceling bookings en masse. South Korea was the main beneficiary, with a 50 percent increase of tourists year over year in the protest's aftermath.

As a 32-year-old Chinese woman from Beijing told me, "Vietnam is like China 30 years ago; I have no interest in visiting. I will go to Europe, Indonesia, or South Korea instead." Response from Chinese tourists to Vietnam has been lukewarm. The country does not have the same temples, beaches, and shopping that Indonesia, Thailand, and South Korea hold.

Manufacturing is also starting to reach a cap there because of the weak infrastructure. Apparel and footwear firms relocated to the country because of salaries one-fourth to one-half that of China—but the lack of ports and number of defects have made many companies rethink their relocation strategy. One American furniture company told me it had to reshore to China operations from Vietnam because the number of defects was too high and the logistics too slow.

Although inflation is down to an acceptable 5 percent, down from the 20 to 30 percent of the previous few years, which causes shopkeepers to prefer American greenbacks in transactions, and the country remains a good manufacturing base for light industry, Vietnam has alienated itself from China and still has rocky relations with the United States. Unless it can maintain a low inflationary environment, improve infrastructure, and ensure safety for Chinese tourists and factories, growth will be slower than in previous years.

❧

Despite China being its third-largest trading partner through the first quarter of 2013 after Japan and the United States, Filipino President Benigno S. Aquino III decided to protest pugnaciously Chinese expansion into the Spratly Islands, which the Philippines claims as its own, and which holds lots of oil reserves.

Like Vietnam, the Philippines has decided to take an aggressive stance to rising Chinese influence in the South China Sea. Unlike Vietnam, the Philippines has extremely tight relations with America so will directly benefit from moving toward the States. Aquino signed in 2013 accords to allow American troops to rotate through the Philippines for joint exercises for the first time since 1992, when America abandoned its Filipino bases.

I used to live in the Philippines in the 1990s, where I taught English literature and economic development at Trinity College of Quezon City (now named Trinity University of Asia). Many of my students told me they considered the Philippines America's fifty-first state. Indeed, all things American seemed to do well there, from TGI Fridays restaurants to American music and clothing brands.

As a direct result of Aquino's aggressive stance, the number of annual tourists from China to the Philippines has dropped a whopping 70 percent in 2013 to 200,000 and is unlikely to rebound anytime soon.

However, I don't see this as a high risk of a bloody tussle with the Philippines in the same way I am concerned about Vietnam and Japan. There is not the same historical mutual suspicion on both sides—in fact, it was a retired high-ranking commodore in the Filipino navy who suggested to me early on in my studies for me to dedicate myself to studying China.

It is, however, likely that tension will continue—China wants to flex its muscles, and the Philippines wants to gain from a closer alliance with the United States. But the riskier flash points are Japan and Vietnam.

China's rise is not a zero-sum game with its neighbors—countries that take the tack of forging closer relations with the country, such as Indonesia and Cambodia, have the opportunity to benefit from increased trade and to attract more tourists. Other nations, such as Vietnam and Sri Lanka, have the opportunity to attract more manufacturing away from China to their countries if they can ensure a stable labor pool and political system.

That said, many Southeast Asian nations are being caught between muscle flexing between China and the United States and being forced to choose sides—the smarter path would be to follow that of Indonesia and Singapore and maintain good relations with both sides.

EPILOGUE

When I first started sharing my ideas for this book, several people challenged me—they did not think Chinese firms had the capability to innovate. They pointed to rampant piracy, a lack of creativity in the education system, and heavy-handed regulation that stifled innovation. One person scoffed, "You will lose credibility for writing there is innovation in China." Another shrilled I was "just plain wrong" because of something inherently wrong in Chinese culture that prevents innovation.

Others responded less politely.

Yet, just a few months later as I was finishing this manuscript, examples of the new focus on innovation emerging from China seemed to pop up every day, such as Baidu's investments in artificial intelligence or new mobile services Tencent launched. I kept extending my deadline for writing because so many new illustrations popped up until I finally had to put my foot down or else I would never finish.

The world started taking notice of the developments, and Chinese innovation started to become a hot topic rather than relegated to articles of scorn, paralleling America's discourse of Japan's rise in the late 1970s and 1980s.

Charles Riley from CNN wrote a piece criticizing Vice President Joe Biden for saying Chinese innovation did not exist—Riley pointed to handset maker Xiaomi and biotech firm B.G.I., which sequences more DNA than any institution in the world, as examples of Chinese innovation and quoted me liberally.[1] Alibaba expanded into the United States with its website 11 Main, offering wares from small and medium retailers, and bought the remaining 34 percent stake in UCWeb, a popular mobile browser. I was invited to appear on *BBC World News* to discuss emerging Chinese innovation with presenter Alice Baxter.

How fast Chinese firms will be able to move up the value chain and reach stage 3 of the innovation curve, where they innovate for the world, remains uncertain, but one thing does not—they are certainly on their way and are no longer copycatting American and European business models' technologies. Underestimating the fast strides many Chinese firms made as Biden does would be a recipe for long-term disaster for companies, investors, and nations.

"We are going live in 2 minutes," a voice from the control room crackled into my earbud.

I was about to be interviewed by Emily Chang, the Harvard-educated, five-time Emmy Award–winning anchor of *Bloomberg West.* Instead of being next to the host, as I was with Dylan Ratigan two years before, I was going to do the interview from Bloomberg's Shanghai studios in the IFC Mall while Chang hosted from San Francisco.

Earlier as I made my way to the studio, I passed the IFC Mall's Apple Store, the most profitable one per square foot globally. In the same mall was the most profitable Morton's Steakhouse in the world. I realized they stood right in the heart of what one Italian investor told me was a ghost city a decade before in 2003. I wondered what else so many foreign analysts get wrong about China.

Chang had spent years based in Beijing as a correspondent for CNN, so I expected penetrating questioning. She got right to it, explaining to the audience that Alibaba differed dramatically from

American Internet players and then asking, "Do American companies like Amazon and eBay have anything to learn from Alibaba and other Chinese companies?"

I thought to myself, *where to begin* . . .

NOTES

CHAPTER 1 THE INNOVATION CURVE STAGE 1: COPYCAT COMPANIES AND LOW-HANGING FRUIT

1. Mourdoukoutas, Panos. "Why China Cannot Develop Its Own iPhone." *Forbes,* February 1, 2012. http://www.forbes.com/sites/panosmourdou koutas/2012/02/01/why-china-cannot-develop-its-own-iphone/.
2. Needham, Joseph. *Science and Civilisation in China.* 7 vols. Cambridge: Cambridge University Press, 1954–98.
3. Riley, Charles. "Joe Biden Is Wrong. China Does Innovate." CNN Money, May 29, 2014. http://money.cnn.com/2014/05/29/technology/ innovation/biden-china-innovation/index.html.
4. Sass, Stephen L. "Can China Innovate without Dissent?" *New York Times,* January 21, 2014. http://www.nytimes.com/2014/01/22/opinion/ can-china-innovate-without-dissent.html.

CHAPTER 2 THE INNOVATION CURVE STAGE 2: EMERGING INNOVATION

1. Goldkorn, Jeremy. "Groupon: 'Getting It in the Ass' in China." *Tech-Crunch,* April 26, 2011. http://techcrunch.epuls.net/2011/04/26/ groupon-getting-it-in-the-ass-in-china/.
2. Jullens, John. "Can China Innovate?" *Global Perspective* (blog). *Strategy+ business,* February 4, 2014. http://www.strategy-business.com/blog/Can-China-Innovate?gko=d49f3.
3. Stevenson-Yang, Anne. "China Innovation: Statements." *Economist,* November 12, 2013. http://www.economist.com/debate/days/view/ 1037/print.

CHAPTER 3 THE INNOVATION CURVE STAGE 2 CONTINUED: INNOVATION FOR CHINA, BIOTECHNOLOGY, AND HEALTH CARE

1. Wadhwa, Vivek. "Chinese Can Innovate—But China Can't." LinkedIn, November 14, 2013. http://www.linkedin.com/today/post/article/20131114180931-8451-chinese-can-innovate-but-china-can-t.

CHAPTER 4 THE INNOVATION CURVE STAGE 3: INNOVATION FOR THE WORLD

1. Laguatan, Ted. "China: A Superpower with No Moral Principles?" *No Limitations* (blog). *Inquirer,* June 11, 2013. http://globalnation.inquirer.net/77233/china-a-superpower-with-no-moral-principles.

CHAPTER 6 THE END OF BLING

1. Gu, Wei. "At China's Biggest Yacht Show, the Party Feel Fizzles." *China Real Time* (blog). *Wall Street Journal,* March 31, 2014. http://blogs.wsj.com/chinarealtime/2014/03/31/at-chinas-biggest-yacht-show-the-party-feel-fizzles/.

CHAPTER 7 CHINA'S EXPANDING CONSUMER CLASS

1. Fincher, Leta Hong. *Leftover Women: The Resurgence of Gender Inequality in China.* Asian Arguments. New York: Zed Books, 2014.
2. Banerjee, Abhijit V., and Esther Duflo. *Poor Economics: A Radical Rethinking of the Way to Fight Global Poverty.* New York: PublicAffairs, 2011.

CHAPTER 9 FOOD SAFETY: FROM CHICKEN TO COFFEE

1. According to Wine Australia, www.smh.com.au/business/australian-wine-sales-to-china-plummet-20140416-36r5i.html.

2. "Mondelez Profit Disappoints, 2014 Outlook above Street View." *Reuters,* February 12, 2014. http://www.reuters.com/article/2014/02/12/monde lez-results-idUSL2N0LC1N820140212.

CHAPTER 10

1. www.cambodiainvestment.gov.kh/investment-enviroment/investment-trend.html.

EPILOGUE

1. Riley, Charles. "Joe Biden Is Wrong. China Does Innovate." CNN Money, May 29, 2014. http://money.cnn.com/2014/05/29/technology/ innovation/biden-china-innovation/index.html.

ACKNOWLEDGMENTS

Writing a book is the culmination of many years of help, support, and advice from many people. To all who have mentored me and pushed me to my limits, thank you.

To my colleagues at the China Market Research Group, thank you for helping contribute to the culture that makes CMR such a great place to work—I love working alongside such bright and passionate people who strive for excellence for ourselves and clients.

I would particularly like to thank my colleagues Ben Cavender and James Roy for shouldering more responsibility on client projects while I was off writing. More than anyone, James gave invaluable feedback on the book.

Last, I would like to thank my wife, Jessica, and my son, Tom, for motivating me to be better.

INDEX